Microsoft Word VBA Guidebook

Second Edition

by Allen L. Wyatt

Microsoft Word VBA Guidebook, Second Edition

Published by:

    Sharon Parq Associates, Inc.
    PO Box 794
    Orem, UT 84059

All contents copyright © 2013 by Sharon Parq Associates, Inc. All rights reserved. No part of this document or the related files may be reproduced or transmitted in any form, by any means (electronic, photocopying, recording, or otherwise) without the prior written permission of the publisher.

For information on purchasing, distributing, or reselling books published by Sharon Parq Associates, Inc., please visit our website (www.SharonParq.com) or call 801-607-2035. Our books are also available through select online resellers such as Amazon.

ISBN: 978-1-61359-197-0 (printed book)
ISBN: 978-1-61359-198-7 (e-book)
ISBN: 978-1-61359-199-4 (e-book on CD-ROM)

Produced and published in the United States of America

Revision history:

    4 May 2011: First published
    3 July 2013: Second edition

Limit of Liability and Disclaimer of Warranty: The publisher has used its best efforts in preparing this book, and the information provided herein is provided "as is." Sharon Parq Associates, Inc., makes no representation or warranties with respect to the accuracy or completeness of the contents of this book and specifically disclaims any implied warranties of merchantability or fitness for any particular purpose and shall in no event be liable for any loss of profit or any other commercial damage, including but not limited to special, incidental, consequential, or other damages.

Trademarks: This book identifies product names and services known to be trademarks, registered trademarks, or service marks of their respective holders. They are used throughout this book in an editorial fashion only. In addition, terms suspected of being trademarks, registered trademarks, or service marks have been appropriately capitalized, although Sharon Parq Associates, Inc., cannot attest to the accuracy of this information. Use of a term in this book should not be regarded as affecting the validity of any trademark, registered trademark, or service mark. Sharon Parq Associates, Inc., is not associated with any product or vendor mentioned in this book.

Internet Addresses. This book includes various Internet addresses, including URLs and e-mail addresses. These addresses are believed to be valid addresses at the time of writing. Due to the fluid nature of the Internet, it is possible that some addresses may become invalid at any time. All addresses are provided for the convenience of the reader, but no address is guaranteed to be valid or still useful to the reader at the time of reading.

Content Overview

	Introduction xiii
1.	Introducing Macros in Word... 1
2.	Elements of Macros.. 15
3.	Naming Considerations.. 43
4.	Understanding the VBA Environment 55
5.	Managing Macros 73
6.	Using VBA's Built-In Functions 85
7.	Controlling Program Flow 107
8.	Using Data Structures 123
9.	Getting Input for Your Macro 131
10.	Working with a Document 147
11.	Working with Selections and Ranges 169
12.	Working with Tables 183
13.	Searching and Replacing 191
14.	Working with Non-Document Files..................................... 201
15.	Debugging and Error Handling... 219
	Index 237

About the Author

Allen Wyatt, an internationally recognized expert in small computer systems, has been working in the computer and publishing industries for more than three decades. He has written more than 50 books explaining many different facets of working with computers, as well as numerous magazine articles. His books have covered topics ranging from working with programming languages to using application software to using operating systems. Through the written word, Allen has helped millions of readers learn how to better use computers.

Besides writing books, Allen has helped educate thousands of individuals through seminars and lectures about computers. He has presented complex topics to audiences throughout the United States as well as throughout Mexico and Costa Rica. His books, which often form the basis of his presentations, have been translated into many languages, including Chinese, Dutch, French, German, Greek, Italian, Japanese, Korean, Polish, Russian, and Spanish.

Allen is the president of Sharon Parq Associates, Inc., a computer and publishing services company located in Orem, Utah. Besides writing books and technical materials, he publishes a series of online newsletters and oversees the development of the Tips.Net family of websites (www.tips.net).

> Allen Wyatt
> Sharon Parq Associates, Inc.
> PO Box 794
> Orem, UT 84059
>
> allen@sharonparq.com

Detailed Table of Contents

Introduction xiii
   Who Did I Write this Book For? xiv
   What Does this Book Cover? xv
   What Doesn't this Book Cover? xv
   Where Do You Go from Here? xvi
   A Word about WordTips xvi

1. Introducing Macros in Word 1
   Understanding VBA 1
      Introducing the Visual Basic Editor 2
      Displaying the Developer Tab 2
   How to Enable Macros 5
   Creating Macros 7
      Recording a Macro 7
      Writing a Macro from Scratch 9
   Running Macros 10
   Editing Macros 11
   Deleting Macros 13

2. Elements of Macros 15
   Projects and Modules 16
   Understanding Procedures 17
      Subroutines 18
      Functions 19
      Procedure Scope 21

Word VBA Guidebook

      Adding Comments 22
      Continuing Lines 23
      Variables and Operators 24
            Understanding Data Types 25
                  The Date Data Type 26
                  The Object Data Type 27
                  The Variant Data Type 27
            Understanding Operators 27
                  Arithmetic Operators 28
                  Comparison Operators 28
                  Logical Operators 30
                  String Operators 32
      Using Objects and Collections 32
            Word's Object Model 33
            Grouping Similar Objects Together 36
            Assigning Objects to Variables 37
      Understanding Object Members 38
            Doing Operations with Methods 38
            Working with Properties 38
            Making Sense of Members 40
      VBA Constants 41
            Using Literal Constants 41
            Creating Symbolic Constants 41
            Word's Enumerations 42

3. Naming Considerations 43
      Naming Macros 43
      Renaming Macros 44
      Where Macros are Stored 45
            Specifying a Location when Recording a Macro 46
            Specifying a Location when Creating a Macro from Scratch 47
      Event Handlers 49
      Automatic Macros 51
      Changing Built-In Word Commands 53

4. Understanding the VBA Environment 55
      Displaying the Visual Basic Editor 55
      Parts of the Environment 57

	The Menu Bar	57
	The Toolbar	59
	The Project Explorer	60
	The Properties Window	61
	The Code Window	62
	The Immediate Window	64
Getting Help		65
	Searching for Help	66
	Navigating the Help System	67
Customizing How VBA Works		67
	Program Options	68
	Project Properties	69
Quitting the Visual Basic Editor		70

5. Managing Macros 73

Adding Macros to Word's Interface 73
    Adding Macros to the Quick Access Toolbar 74
    Adding Macros to Ribbon Tabs 76
Creating Shortcut Keys for Macros 78
Using the Organizer 80
Exporting Macros 81
Importing Macros 83

6. Using VBA's Built-In Functions 85

The Benefits of Functions 85
Date and Time Functions 86
    How VBA Stores Times and Dates 87
    Determining Today's Date 88
    Determining the Current Time 89
    Getting Both the Time and Date 89
    Extracting Part of the Date 90
    Displaying a Weekday Name 91
    Extracting Part of the Time 91
    Differences between Two Dates 92
    Deriving a Date 93
String Functions 93
    Comparing Strings 94
    Converting Strings 95

Converting the Case of a String 96
Converting Characters to Values 96
Converting Values to Characters 96
Converting a String to a Number 97
Converting a Number to a String 97
Creating Strings 98
Other String Functions 98
Finding the Length of a String 99
Strings within Strings 99
Extracting the Ends and Middle of a String 100
Math Functions 100
Extracting an Integer 101
Generating Random Numbers 101
Determining the Sign of a Number 103
Positive Values 104
Formatting 105

7. Controlling Program Flow 107
Conditional Execution 107
If ... Then 108
Formatting If ... Then Structures 110
Using Not With If...Then 111
Select Case 112
Switch 113
Looping Structures 114
For Loop 114
Incrementing the Loop Counter 115
Nesting a For Loop 116
For Each Loop 117
Do Loop 118
The First Time Through 118
Exiting a Loop 119
While Loops 120
GoTo 121

8. Using Data Structures 123
Understanding Arrays 123
Setting Up an Array 124

Detailed Table of Contents

      Changing Arrays on the Fly 125
      Multidimensional Arrays 126
  Getting Information about an Array 127
  Starting to Count 127
  User-Defined Data Types 128

9. Getting Input for Your Macro 131
  Creating a Message Box 132
      The Message 132
      The Title 134
      Icons, Buttons, and Responses 135
          Changing Icons 135
          Changing Buttons 136
          Combining Buttons and Icons 137
          User Feedback 137
  Getting User Input 138
      The Prompt 139
      The Title 140
      Default Input 140
      Screen Coordinates 141
  Built-In Dialog Boxes 141
      Available Dialog Boxes 142
      Displaying Dialog Boxes 143
      Accessing Dialog Box Settings 144

10. Working with a Document 147
  The Document Object 147
      Creating New Documents 148
      Opening Existing Documents 149
      Getting to a Document's Name 151
  Accessing Paragraphs 152
      Adding Paragraphs 152
      Accessing Paragraphs 153
      Deleting Paragraphs 154
  Accessing Styles 155
  Using Explicit Formatting 156
      Formatting Paragraphs 156
      Formatting Characters 159

Using Bookmarks 161
    Adding Bookmarks 162
    Accessing Existing Bookmarks 163
    Deleting Bookmarks 165
Saving Documents 165
    The Close Method 165
    The Save Method 166
    The SaveAs Method 166

11. Working with Selections and Ranges 169
Creating a Selection 170
Finding Information about the Selection 172
    General Information 172
    Selection Information 173
    Table Information 175
Editing the Selection 176
    Adding Text 176
    Inserting Paragraphs 177
    Deleting Text 177
    Collapsing the Selection 178
Creating a Range 178
Editing a Range 179
    Adding Text 179
    Replacing Text 180
    Deleting Text 181

12. Working with Tables 183
Creating Tables 183
Changing Table Structure 185
    Deleting Rows and Columns 185
    Adding Rows and Columns 186
    Merging and Splitting Cells 186
Changing Table Characteristics 187
    Changing Row Height and Column Width 188
    Changing Formatting 188
Adding Information to Tables 189
Deleting Tables 190

13. Searching and Replacing 191
Finding Things 191
Find Properties 193
Executing a Search 195
Using Find to Modify Your Document 196
Replacing Things 197

14. Working with Non-Document Files 201
File Types 201
Text Files 202
Foreign File Formats 203
Import/Export Formats 204
File Basics 204
Opening a File 205
Handling File Errors 206
Reading Data Files 206
Closing Files 207
Types of File Access 208
Sequential Files 208
Reading ASCII Text Files 208
Writing to ASCII Text Files 210
Reading Delimited Text Files 211
Writing Delimited Text Files 212
Random-Access Files 212
Record Variables: User-Defined Types 212
Opening Random-Access Files 214
Reading Records from Random-access Files 215
Writing Records to Random-Access Files 215
Binary Files 216
Opening Files for Binary Access 216
Reading from Binary Access Files 217
Writing to Binary-Access Files 217
Updating the Current Position in a Binary File 217
Determining the Current Position in a Binary File 218

15. Debugging and Error Handling 219
What Are Bugs? 219
Syntax-Related Errors 220

Logic-Related Errors	220
Operation-Related Errors	221
Why are Bugs a Problem?	221
Keeping Bugs Out	222
What is Debugging?	224
Getting Rid of Bugs	224
Single Stepping	226
What's Its Value?	226
Stepping By Procedures	229
Breakpoints	230
Setting a Breakpoint	230
Debugging Using Breakpoints	231
Watch Expressions	233
Breaking on Watches	234
Editing a Watch	235

Index 237

Introduction

Microsoft Word is the best-selling, most-used word processing software in the world. That is in no small part because of the power inherent in the program. Many people are content to use the features that Word makes available through the program's ribbons and tools. Others, however, know that the real power of Word is in its extensible nature.

A program is considered *extensible* if you can extend it in some manner. Word's capabilities can be extended through the use of its powerful macro programming language. That's what this book is about—using the VBA (Visual Basic for Applications) language within Word. I wrote *Microsoft Word VBA Guidebook* because I could not find a good entry-level guide anywhere for people wanting to learn how to program Word macros. I updated *Microsoft Word VBA Guidebook* to this second edition to provide an updated, enhanced version of the book that reflects the newer versions of Word.

Some people are a bit skittish when it comes to macros. They get the same feeling that they get when they go into unfamiliar territory or venture into some new experience. It is easy to feel that way, but there really is no need—macros can be as simple or as challenging as you want them to be. You can work through this book at your own pace, trying out the pieces and parts of VBA that interest you and that make your use of Word better than before.

Who Did I Write this Book For?

Every book is written with assumptions about you, the reader. This book is no different; in writing it I tried to make as few assumptions as possible. Even so, it is best to lay out those assumptions so you can figure out if you are the person I had in mind as I was writing.

First, I assume that you are naturally inquisitive—that you like to "poke around" under the hood, so to speak. I enjoy seeing what this command does or that feature accomplishes, and I believe you are the same way. That adventuresome spirit is helpful in learning, particularly in learning a topic as expansive (and, to some people, daunting) as macro programming.

I also assume that you know a good deal about how to use Word. Before delving into macros, it is a good idea to have more than a passing familiarity with the major parts of the program. You should know how to open, edit, and save documents. It doesn't hurt to know how Word views the relationship between text and formatting and how formatting is encapsulated in styles. You should know how to work with tables, how to define bookmarks, and what constitutes a paragraph in a Word document.

It's a plus if you can figure out why your text doesn't always look the way you want it to and what you can do about it. You know the difference between an endnote and a footnote and you know how to add both of them to your documents. In short, you should already know your way around Word, from a user's perspective, before you seek to extend the program through macros.

Another assumption is that you are using one of the latest versions of Word— Word 2007, Word 2010, or Word 2013. This book was written with you in mind. While VBA (the programming language used in Word) has been around since Word 97, the interface and features of Word, itself, were greatly changed starting with Word 2007. All of the examples and screen shots provided in this book were created and grabbed with these three latest versions in mind. (Virtually all of the screen shots were taken in Word 2013 running on a Windows 8 system. You'll also find a few shots taken with either Word 2007, on a Vista system, or Word 2010, on a Windows 7 system.)

Finally, I assume that you aren't afraid to try things. You'll get plenty of opportunity to try things out as you work through this book.

What Does this Book Cover?

In a word (no pun intended), this book covers a lot. I've tried to cover everything you'll need to know to start programming your own macros and editing the macros you may get from others. That means I've included everything I consider to be basic and elemental in nature, but I don't just stop there—I also include quite a bit that you will find challenging as you expand your understanding.

If you are brand new to macros (you've never worked in the Visual Basic Editor before), then you'll want to make sure you read the first three chapters in order. They are foundational to everything else you may learn about macros. This is particularly true about Chapter 2, *Elements of Macros,* which covers a ton of ground about VBA in the Word environment. (You'll definitely want to return to and refer to that chapter over and over again.)

The rest of the chapters in the book cover well-defined topics that expand the basic information you pick up in the first three chapters. You can, if you desire, read them in any order you want, as your programming needs pull you this way or that way. Of particular interest to those wishing to process documents with macros will be 10 through 13 which focus on using Word's object model. (The object model is key to understanding how you access parts of your Word document from within your macro.)

What Doesn't this Book Cover?

The topic of macros is so expansive that it is impossible for a single book to cover everything related to the topic. There are a few things that this book does not cover, but they are largely advanced or esoteric items related to macros.

The two primary things not covered are creating digital signatures for your macros and how to create your own add-ins. I also don't really get into the

XML structure of Word's documents and how you can use XML to modify the user interface. All of those are topics better left to treatment in other books.

Finally, I don't really cover how to create custom user forms (custom dialog boxes). VBA has a rich ability to create them, but they seemed—at least to me—to be beyond the needs of who I envision as the average reader of this book. If you want to learn about the, consider a good programmer's reference for Visual Basic; it shares the same capabilities as VBA.

Where Do You Go from Here?

If you need more information about programming macros in Word, I strongly suggest that you consider *WordTips: The Macros*. This e-book, currently in its sixth edition, contains hundreds of tips, tricks, and ideas on how you can use macros in ways you may never have thought of. It is a great companion to *Microsoft Word VBA Guidebook,* providing the "next step" in programming prowess you want.

If you decide you want your own copy of this great book, you can find it here:

```
http://store.tips.net
```

A Word about WordTips

I've been using Word since its earliest days, back when it only ran in a DOS environment. (It wasn't difficult then—Windows hadn't even been thought of yet.) I have worked in large publishing corporations, spearheading their conversion efforts to Microsoft Word. In the mid-1990s I wrote several books about how to use Word, and early in March 1997 I started a free weekly newsletter devoted to tips and ideas on how to use the program better.

That weekly newsletter, *WordTips,* is still running strong. It is published every Saturday morning, and you can subscribe for free. Many of the tips published in the newsletter involve the use of macros and they can be instructive for your own efforts in extending what Word can do.

More information (including thousands and thousands of online tips) is available at the *WordTips* website:

```
http://wordribbon.tips.net
```

If you decide you want to subscribe to the newsletter (again, it is free), you can do so at the right side of any page on the website.

Introducing Macros in Word

When you start to understand the word "macro," you begin to see that it is a word with a rich history, but also one that doesn't always have a good reputation—at least in the programming community. You see, macros are often viewed as nothing more than a series of memorized steps to be performed over and over again.

While Microsoft built into Word the ability to record a series of steps so you can perform them again and again, macros in Word are much more than the pejorative term that programmers often envision. In this chapter you'll start to see why this is the case as you create your first macros. Specifically, you'll discover the following:

- Why Microsoft chose VBA as its macro language
- How to configure your system to allow macros
- The two major ways of creating macros
- How to run, edit, and delete macros

Understanding VBA

In the early days of Microsoft Word, the program used a macro language known as WordBASIC. Based upon the BASIC programming language, WordBASIC allowed users to not only record a series of keystrokes, but also to create full-blown programs within the Word environment, based upon traditional programming practices.

Starting with Word 97 (and continuing through all versions since then), Microsoft has used Visual Basic for Applications (VBA) as its macro programming language. This language is much more powerful than WordBASIC ever could be. It is still based upon the BASIC programming language, but VBA is essentially a subset of Microsoft's Visual Basic object-oriented programming language.

One huge advantage of VBA is that it is standardized across all of Microsoft's Office applications. This means that you can learn VBA for one application (such as Word) and have a great head-start on using the language in other applications in the Office suite (such as Excel). It is interesting to note that VBA has been so successful and proved so useful that some other companies, besides Microsoft, have adopted it as the macro programming language for their applications.

Introducing the Visual Basic Editor

When you work with VBA programs, you do so in what is termed the Visual Basic Editor. This is a special place in which macros can be worked with in Word. (You don't work with macros in the document window; you must work with them in the Visual Basic Editor.) You'll find a full discussion of the Visual Basic Editor in Chapter 4, but it's good for you to have a brief introduction right now, simply because the moment you start using macros you'll run into the Visual Basic Editor.

For now, simply display the Visual Basic Editor by starting Word and then pressing ALT+F11. Your document window stays on the screen, but a whole new screen appears. This is the editor, as shown in Figure 1-1.

Displaying the Developer Tab

In order to make tools and features available to users, Word utilizes what is generally known as a *ribbon interface*. This interface uses a series of tabs, at the top of the screen, that show the various tools available. You can change which tools you see by selecting the different tabs.

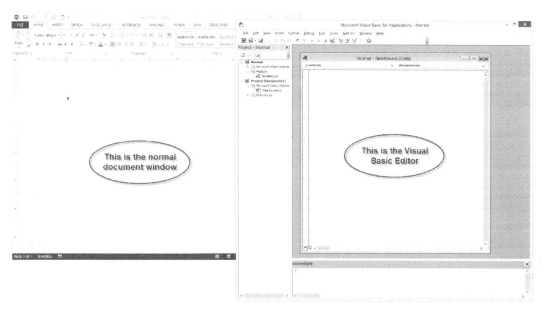

Figure 1-1. *The Visual Basic Editor is where you do your work with macros.*

For those working with macros, one tab that is most helpful to display is the Developer tab. This tab should be visible near the right side of the ribbon.

If you cannot see the Developer tab on the ribbon, then you need to turn it on so that it is displayed. How you turn on the Developer tab depends on the version of Word you are using. If you are using Word 2010 or Word 2013, follow these steps:

1. Click the File tab of the ribbon.
2. Click Options. Word displays the Word Options dialog box.
3. At the left side of the dialog box choose Customize Ribbon.

4. At the right side of the dialog box, make sure the check box at the left of the Developer tab entry is selected, as shown in Figure 1-2.
5. Click OK.

If you are using Word 2007, follow these steps instead:

1. Click the Office button and then click Word Options. Word displays the Word Options dialog box.
2. Make sure the Popular option is selected at the left of the dialog box.
3. Ensure there is a check mark in the Show Developer Tab in Ribbon check box. (See Figure 1-3.)
4. Click OK.

With the Developer tab displayed on the ribbon, you are almost ready to jump right into the deep end of the pool and start creating macros.

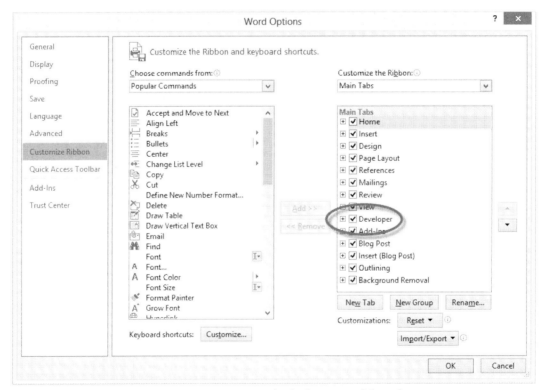

Figure 1-2. *You can control whether any of the tabs are displayed on the ribbon, including the Developer tab.*

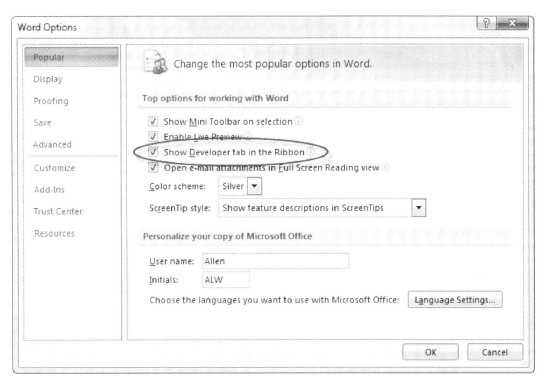

Figure 1-3. *In Word 2007 you control the display of the Developer tab of the ribbon by using the Word Options dialog box.*

How to Enable Macros

When you first use Word, or if you use it for a while without ever having used macros, the program is configured to automatically disable macros. In order for you to start working with macros, it is a good idea to enable them on your system.

There are two ways you can display the Trust Center. If you have the Developer tab of the ribbon available (as described in the previous section), display the Developer tab and click the Macro Security tool in the Code group.

The second way to display the Trust Center varies involves following these steps:

Word VBA Guidebook

1. Display the Word Options dialog box. (In Word 2007 click the Office button and then click Word Options. In Word 2010 and Word 2013 display the File tab of the ribbon and then click Options.)
2. Click Trust Center at the left of the dialog box.
3. Click Trust Center Settings.
4. Make sure Macro Settings is selected at the left of the dialog box.

Once the Trust Center is displayed (as shown in Figure 1-4) you can select a security setting that allows you to run your macros.

The Trust Center has four settings for macro security:

- **Disable all macros without notification.** All macros and security alerts about macros are automatically disabled.
- **Disable all macros with notification.** Macros are disabled, but a security alert is displayed to allow you to enable macros on a case-by-case basis.

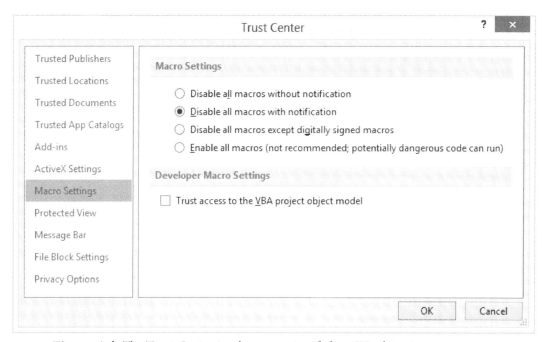

Figure 1-4. *The Trust Center is where you specify how Word treats your macros.*

- **Disable all macros except digitally signed macros.** Non-signed macros are disabled, but a security alert is displayed to allow their enabling. If the macro is digitally signed and from a publisher you trust, it is automatically enabled.
- **Enable all macros.** All macros, regardless of source, are automatically enabled.

As you are developing your own macros, the best balance of permissiveness and security is the second options, Disable All Macros with Notification. Select this option and then click OK. You are now ready to start creating your own macros.

Creating Macros

It makes sense that before you can use macros to enhance how you work with Word, you need to create the macros that you'll use. Word provides two ways that you can create macros—you can either record a macro or you can write one from scratch.

Recording a Macro

Most people cut their teeth on macro programming by recording a series of actions so the actions can later be executed again. For instance, let's say that you want to record the steps required to replace all instances of the word "Notice" (capitalized as shown) with the phrase "Take Note" and for the replacement text to be both bold and in red. You could easily record these actions in this manner:

1. Make sure the Developer tab of the ribbon is displayed.
2. In the Code group, click Record Macro. Word displays the Record Macro dialog box, as shown in Figure 1-5.
3. Click OK. Note that the Record Macro tool, in the Code group on the Developer tab, changes to a Stop Recording tool.
4. Press **Ctrl+H**. Word displays the Replace tab of the Find and Replace dialog box.

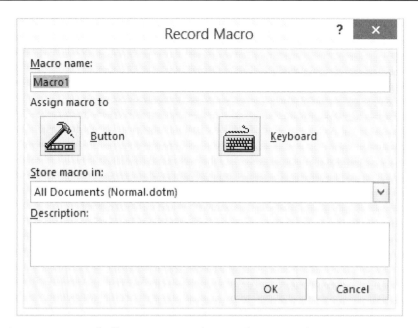

Figure 1-5. Word allows you to easily record a series of actions as a macro.

5. In the Find What box enter what you want to search for: **Notice**
6. In the Replace With box enter what you want the replacement text to be: **Take Note**
7. Click the More button, if it is available.
8. Make sure the Match Case check box is selected.
9. Click once in the Replace With box so that the insertion point is within the box.
10. Click Format | Font. Word displays the Replace Font dialog box.
11. In the Font Style area choose Bold.
12. Using the Font Color drop-down list, choose red.
13. Click OK.
14. Click Replace All. Word makes all the replacements in the document.
15. Close any dialog boxes that are still open.
16. On the Developer tab of the ribbon, click Stop Recording.

That's it. Word dutifully recorded all the steps between when you started the macro recorder and when you stopped it—steps 4 through 15. The macro was saved using the name visible in the step 2, in the Record Macro dialog box. You can "replay" the steps at any time, simply by running the macro again. (We'll get to how you actually run macros in just a moment.)

When talking about recording macros, I should state that the recorder only records discrete actions—steps you take. It does not record any mouse movements. (However, when you click on something using the mouse—as you did several times in the above steps—those don't count as "mouse movements." They are discrete actions that are recorded by the macro recorder.)

Writing a Macro from Scratch

While recording a macro can provide a quick way to begin using a macro, a much more powerful approach is to write a macro from scratch. As long as you can visualize what you want the macro to do, you can use the Visual Basic Editor to write the steps that are necessary to accomplish your task.

To create a macro from scratch, follow these steps:

1. Make sure the Developer tab of the ribbon is displayed.
2. In the Code group click the Macros tool. Word displays the Macros dialog box, shown in Figure 1-6.
3. Using the Macros In drop-down list (near the bottom of the dialog box), select where you want your new macro stored. Select Normal.dotm (Global Template) if you want your macro available in all documents; select a different template if you want the macro available only with that particular document template. You can even assign a macro to a specific document.
4. In the Macro Name box, type a descriptive name you want assigned to the macro you are writing. (Make sure the name doesn't have any spaces in it.)
5. Optionally, you can enter information in the Description box.
6. Click on Create. The Visual Basic Editor is started and you can write your macro.

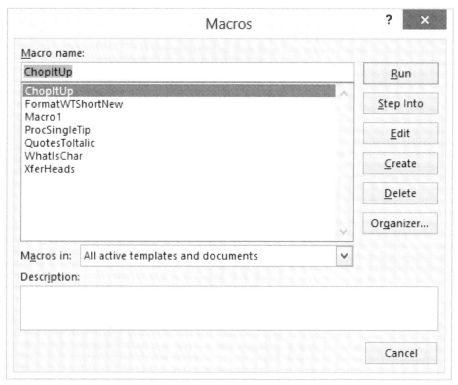

Figure 1-6. The Macros dialog box is used to manage the macros that Word knows about on your system.

7. When you are through, close the editor window by selecting the Close and Return to Microsoft Word option from the File menu, or by pressing ALT+Q.

Running Macros

Running a macro is easy to do; you use the same Macros dialog box introduced in the previous section. If you know which macro you want to run, just follow these steps:

1. Make sure the Developer tab of the ribbon is displayed.
2. In the Code group click the Macros tool. Word displays the Macros dialog box, shown in Figure 1-6.

3. In the list of macros displayed in the dialog box, click once on the macro you want to run.

4. Click the Run button. Word closes the dialog box and runs the macro you specified.

As an example, let's suppose that you want to run the macro you recorded earlier in this chapter. If you accepted the default name for the macro (shown in Figure 1-4), you can see that name in the Macros dialog box (Figure 1-6). All you need to do is click the macro and then click Run. The search and replace operation is again performed on your document.

While using the Macros dialog box to run macros may be easy, it can also get monotonous if you run macros quite often. If you have macros you want to run over and over, it may make more sense to have them assigned to either a keyboard shortcut or to a button somewhere on the ribbon. Once assigned to a shortcut key or a button, you can then run the macro by simply invoking the shortcut key or clicking on the button. How you assign macros to shortcut keys or ribbon buttons is discussed fully in Chapter 5.

Editing Macros

Just as surely as day follows night, at some point you'll need to edit a macro you previously recorded or wrote from scratch. Remember that all editing of macros occurs using the Visual Basic Editor. To edit an existing macro, all you need to do is follow these steps:

1. Make sure the Developer tab of the ribbon is displayed.

2. In the Code group click the Macros tool. Word displays the Macros dialog box, shown in Figure 1-6.

3. In the list of macros displayed in the dialog box, click once on the macro you want to edit.

4. Click the Edit button. Word closes the dialog box and displays the Visual Basic Editor.

5. Make any changes desired in your macro.

6. When you are through, close the editor by selecting the Close and Return to Microsoft Word option from the File menu or by pressing ALT+Q.

As an example, let's say that you want to edit the macro you recorded earlier in this chapter. You display the Macros dialog box and see your macro (Macro1) listed among those on your system. You click the macro name once and then click Edit. Word displays the Visual Basic Editor with your macro displayed in the code window, as shown in Figure 1-7.

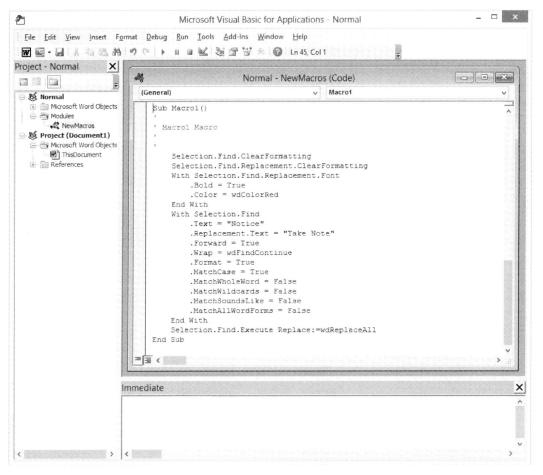

Figure 1-7. The Visual Basic Editor shows your macro in the Code window.

Editing an existing macro is very much like creating a new macro from scratch. The only difference is your starting point—when editing an existing macro you can see and change the code that you previously created for the macro.

You can edit information in the Visual Basic Editor using many of the same editing techniques you use when working with Word documents. For instance, you can select code in the window and use copy and paste commands to move the code around. You can also use the mundane editing keys (like BACKSPACE and DELETE) to make changes to the code, as necessary.

Deleting Macros

You'll find, over time, that many of the macros that you record or create are used for a specific purpose; they are not intended to be used over and over again for long periods of time. This means that as your needs change, you may have occasion to delete macros. To delete a macro, follow these steps:

1. Make sure the Developer tab of the ribbon is displayed.
2. In the Code group click the Macros tool. Word displays the Macros dialog box, shown in Figure 1-6.
3. From the list of macros, select the macro you want to delete. The Delete button becomes available.
4. Click on Delete.
5. Repeat steps 3 and 4 for each macro you want to delete.
6. Click on Close when finished.

Elements of Macros

When you first look at the programming code in a macro, you may feel lost. Don't worry; this is normal for those just beginning to work with macros. (Come on; admit it—you felt a little overwhelmed when you looked at the code for the first macro you ever recorded, didn't you?) As you spend more time with the actual code stored in macros, those feelings subside and you become more and more comfortable.

As is the case with any programming language, VBA relies upon some fundamental building blocks in any macro. A firm understanding of those building blocks can help you make sense of macros faster and create them easier. This chapter focuses upon those building blocks. Here you'll find information about each of the following:

- How projects and modules are used in macros
- Macro procedures
- Commenting macros
- Breaking up long lines in a macro
- Using objects and collections
- Understanding object methods and properties
- Using variables and operators

Projects and Modules

Visual Basic for Applications is an object-oriented programming language. This means that it understands and works with objects, as is discussed in detail later in this chapter. The highest-level object understood by VBA is known as a *project*.

For the layman non-programmer, the best way to understand a project is as either a document or a template. Each project (hence, each document or template) can contain other objects. Specifically, a project can contain any of the following:

- **Microsoft Word objects.** These are objects such as documents and templates. In a way, this type of object is almost circular, since a project is analogous to a document or template. However, because VBA treats these as objects, you can use programming techniques to access their internal elements, such as paragraphs and words.
- **Modules.** A module (discussed shortly) is a container for a group of related procedures (also discussed shortly). In short, a module contains your VBA programming code.
- **Class modules.** These are a special type of programming code used to define custom objects that can be used elsewhere in your programming. These are used extensively by programmers who understand the intricacies of object-oriented programming.
- **UserForm objects.** A UserForm is a custom dialog box used as in interface to a program. UserForms are considered an advanced topic, well beyond the level of beginning programmers.
- **References.** These are nothing but formal references to other projects. These are necessary when you want to *reference* objects in a different project from the current project.

The easiest way to get a handle on what constitutes a project is to user the Project Explorer, a special area visible within the Visual Basic Editor. (The Project Explorer is covered in more detail in Chapter 4.) Figure 2-1 shows an example of the Project Explorer, which displays projects and the objects within projects in a hierarchical fashion, using a tree representation.

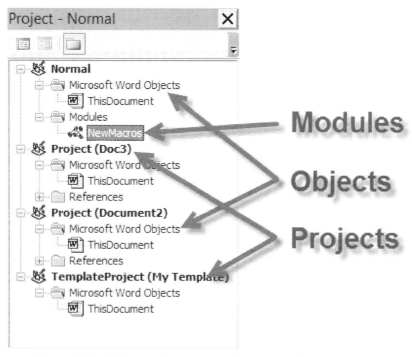

Figure 2-1. *VBA uses the concept of projects and objects extensively. The Project Explorer displays the relationship between these elements.*

For those using VBA, the most common object is known as a module. A *module* is a collection of programming procedures that you create. When you first record a macro, Word places the recording into a module known as NewMacros. By default this module is placed within the Normal project, meaning that it is associated with the Normal template that is loaded with every Word document. You can override where macros are stored, as discussed in Chapter 3.

Understanding Procedures

The simplest definition of a procedure is a logical grouping of programming code used to accomplish one or more related tasks. (That didn't sound too formal, did it?) VBA understands two types of procedures:

- Subroutines
- Functions

Procedures are elemental, meaning that you cannot place procedures within procedures. For instance, you cannot put a subroutine within a function or within another subroutine. You can, however, execute one procedure from another procedure, as is made clear in the following sections.

Subroutines

The first type of programming procedure you can create in VBA is known as a subroutine. For instance, consider the following code:

```
Sub Macro1()
    TestSub
End Sub

Sub TestSub()
    StatusBar = "In the macro"
End Sub
```

This code consists of two subroutines, Macro1 and TestSub. You can tell that these are subroutines because they start, in the first line of each procedure, with the Sub keyword. In fact, you can see that each subroutine is enclosed within two lines—the first declares the name of the subroutine using the Sub keyword and the second ends the subroutine with the End Sub statement.

In this example the Macro1 macro does nothing but call a subroutine (TestSub), which in turn prints a message on the status bar. The subroutine then returns control to the main program.

You can have as many subroutines in your module as you desire. The purpose of each should be to perform common tasks so you don't have to rewrite the same code all the time. Properly used, subroutines can be very powerful.

You can increase the flexibility of your subroutines by passing parameters to them. These parameters can then be acted upon by your subroutine. For instance, consider the following macros:

```
Sub Macro1()
    A = 1
    PrintIt A
End Sub
```

```
Sub PrintIt(x)
    StatusBar = x
End Sub
```

When you run Macro1, it assigns a value to a variable (A) and then passes that variable in a subroutine call to PrintIt. This PrintIt subroutine displays the value of the variable on the status bar and then returns to the calling program.

Notice that the PrintIt subroutine does not use the same variable name that was used when PrintIt was invoked in the Macro1 macro. This is because VBA reassigns the value of x (what the subroutine expects to receive) so that it matches the value of A (what the program is passing to the subroutine). The important thing to remember in passing parameters to subroutines is that your program must pass the same number of parameters as the subroutine expects, and that the parameters must be of matching types and in the proper order. (The proper use of variables is discussed later in this chapter.)

Functions

The second type of procedure you can use in your programming is known as a *function*. The difference between functions and subroutines is that functions can return values, whereas subroutines cannot. Consider the following procedures:

```
Sub Macro1()
    TooMany = TestFunc
    If TooMany Then StatusBar = "Too many pages"
End Sub

Function TestFunc() As Boolean
    TestFunc = False
    If Selection.Information(wdNumberOfPagesInDocument) > 10 Then
        TestFunc = True
    End If
End Function
```

There are two procedures in this code, one subroutine and one function. You already know how to spot the subroutine (see the previous section) and you can probably figure out that the function is named TestFunc. Note that similarly to subroutines, functions are enclosed within two lines that denote the beginning and end of the function. The keyword Function is used to define the function and the statement End Function is used to mark the end of the function.

Take a closer look at how the function is defined in its first line:

```
Function TestFunc() As Boolean
```

The Function keyword indicates you are defining a function and giving it the name TestFunc. Note that after the parentheses you can see the keywords "As Boolean". This means that you are instructing VBA to return, from the TestFunc function, a value that uses the Boolean data type. (Data types are discussed fully later in this chapter.) Now take a look at the body of the function:

```
TestFunc = False
If Selection.Information(wdNumberOfPagesInDocument) > 10 Then
    TestFunc = True
End If
```

Note that a variable named TestFunc is set to either False or True, depending on the condition within the If … Then structure. It isn't the structure that is important at this point; that is explained fully in Chapter 7. What is important is noticing that the code assigns a value to a variable that has the same name as the function itself (TestFunc). It is the value of this variable that is returned, as a Boolean, when the function is completed.

This brings us back to the Macro1 macro. Note that the TestFunc function can appear on the right side of the equal sign. This makes functions very powerful and an important part of any program. VBA executes the function, returns whatever value is appropriate from that function, and assigns it to the variable on the left side of the equal sign (TooMany). The rest of the code in the Macro1 macro then acts upon the value returned.

When you create your own functions, it is often helpful to pass parameters to the function. These parameters can be used either as data that you want the function to act upon or as settings used to control how the function does its work. How you pass parameters to functions is illustrated in the following:

```
Sub Macro1()
    A = 12.3456
    Status.Bar = A & "    " & RoundIt(A)
End Sub

Function RoundIt(X) As Integer
    RoundIt = Int(X + 0.5)
End Function
```

The Macro1 macro defines a number and assigns it to the variable A. It then prints that number and the result of passing the number to the RoundIt function; the output is 12.3456 and 12. Notice that the parameter should be passed to the function within parentheses.

Also notice that the function does not use the same variable name as it was passed. (The variable A is passed to the function when it is invoked; within the function this value is referred to by the variable name X.) This is because VBA reassigns the value of X (what the function needs) so it matches the value of A (what is passed to the function).

VBA allows you to specify multiple parameters to be passed to a function. The parameters simply need to be separated by commas in both the declaration of the function and whenever the function is called. The important thing to remember in passing parameters to functions is that your program must pass the same number of parameters as the function expects, and the parameters must be of matching types and in the proper order.

Procedure Scope

It should be noted that procedures (either subroutines or functions) can have a *scope* declared for them. By scope Microsoft simply means how accessible the procedure is. A procedure can either be public or private.

- A public procedure is accessible from any module in a project.
- A private procedure can be accessed only within the module in which the procedure occurs.

You declare the scope of a procedure by preceding the procedure's declaration with either the word Public or Private. The default scope for a procedure is public, so either of these declarations is exactly the same:

```
Public Sub UpdateMonth()
Sub UpdateMonth()
```

Because VBA assumes that all procedures are public unless declared otherwise, most programmers don't bother with the Public keyword. Instead, they simply use Private in places where they feel it is necessary:

```
Private Function EndCycle(iCycle As Integer) As String
```

You should also note that any subroutine declared Private does not appear in the Macros dialog box. This is because Word assumes that since you've marked it Private, you only want it available to invoke from other procedures in your project, not to be run manually by humans.

Adding Comments

Anyone who has been programming for any length of time can share a common experience: Writing a program, leaving that program for a period of time—perhaps months—and then coming back to the program and forgetting what was happening in the code. It is frustrating to need to go back and "decipher" what you wrote months before in order to make changes to that code.

This same thing can easily happen when you are programming macros; it is easy to forget what your program is doing or why you wrote your program. For this reason, VBA provides a way that you can add comments to your code. The comments are completely ignored by VBA, but they provide a way for you to explain anything about your code that you feel needs explaining.

Here is an example of commenting that was done in a macro:

```
Sub ConvertText()
' Replaces all instances of 'Note' with 'Important!'
' Make sure replacement text is blue

    Selection.Find.ClearFormatting
    Selection.Find.Replacement.ClearFormatting

    'Make replacement text bold, italic, and blue
    With Selection.Find.Replacement.Font
        .Bold = True
        .Italic = True
        .Color = wdColorBlue
    End With

    With Selection.Find       'Set up for the replacing
        .Text = "Note"
        .Replacement.Text = "Important!"
        .Wrap = wdFindContinue
        .Format = True
        .MatchCase = True
```

```
        .MatchWholeWord = True
    End With

    'Perform the replacement
    Selection.Find.Execute Replace:=wdReplaceAll
End Sub
```

Don't get bogged down in what this code actually does; that isn't important at the moment. What is important is the presence of comments within the code. Note any lines that begin with an apostrophe; these are comments. When viewed in the Visual Basic Editor, comments appear as green text so that you can easily tell them apart from the main programming code.

If you examine this code example closely, you'll find that on some lines the apostrophe that denotes the start of a comment begins at the left margin. On some other lines it is indented a bit and on one line the apostrophe is even a few spaces to the right of some real code. The point is that VBA ignores everything after the apostrophe; it is considered a comment meant for human eyes only.

As you are programming, you'll want to make sure that you add comments liberally in your code. Doing so can help you (or others) later remember your thought process as you created your macro.

Continuing Lines

When you are creating a macro, you may run into some very long lines. VBA can handle very long lines easily, but it is usually a pain to scroll the screen left and right to review a line. Some programming languages (Such as C or Perl) allow you to continue program lines simply by pressing ENTER and continuing with the line.

VBA, however, requires a special character sequence to signify that you want to continue the current program line on the next. This sequence consists of a space and an underscore. Consider the following example code:

```
Selection.ParagraphFormat.TabStops.Add Position:=InchesToPoints(2.25),
Alignment:=wdAlignTabDecimal, Leader:=wdTabLeaderSpaces
```

This is a single programming statement that sets a tab stop in the currently selected paragraph. It shows on two lines in this text, but on the screen, in the Visual Basic Editor, it would be a single, very wide line. To see it all, you would need to scroll your screen to the right quite a ways.

A better solution is to add the space and underscore characters strategically within the line. That informs the editor that you are actually creating a single programming statement, but that you are spreading it across multiple lines for the sake of readability. Here's an example:

```
Selection.ParagraphFormat.TabStops.Add _
  Position:=InchesToPoints(2.25), _
  Alignment:=wdAlignTabDecimal, _
  Leader:=wdTabLeaderSpaces
```

Take a look at the right side of the first three lines. The space and underscore at the end of each line signifies that the programming statement continues on the next line. You can use the continuation characters in this way to continue any programming lines you desire. The only thing you need to remember is that you can only use the characters for continuation purposes if you place them between regular tokens or keywords used in the program line. If you place them in the middle of a keyword or in a string (between quote marks), VBA won't know what you intended and may generate an error.

Variables and Operators

In order to operate, most computer programs make some sort of calculation. These calculations are made using variables, which are the building blocks of the calculating portion of your program. Just like different parts of a building may require different sizes of bricks, different portions of your programs require different types of variables.

In the following sections you learn about the different types of variables and operators you can use in VBA. One of the marks of a good programmer is the ability to match the right data type with the proper operator to produce the precise result desired. These sections teach you the fundamentals you need to increase your skills in this area.

Understanding Data Types

Variables are nothing but a storage space for values. If you prefer real-world analogies, you can think of them as containers that hold information. They are called variables because their contents can vary, meaning they can be changed. Just as you can change what is stored inside a drinking glass, you can change what is stored within a variable.

Variables come in different types (often called data types) so you can properly handle different types of information. Because VBA provides different types of variables you can use in your programs, you must learn about them so you can use them effectively. These are the data types that VBA supports:

- **Byte.** A numeric variable within the range of 0 to 255.
- **Boolean.** A variable with two possible values: True (-1) or False (0).
- **Integer.** A numeric variable designed for whole numbers in the range of -32,768 to 32,767.
- **Long.** A numeric variable designed for very large whole numbers.
- **Currency.** A numeric variable designed for calculations involving monetary values.
- **Single.** A numeric variable designed for single-precision floating-point values; accurate to about six or seven decimal places.
- **Double.** A numeric variable designed for double-precision floating-point values; accurate to about 15 decimal places.
- **Date.** A numeric variable designed to represent a date and time as a real number. The value to the left of the decimal point is the date, and that portion to the right of the decimal point is the time.
- **String.** A variable that can contain any type of text or character you desire. You can assign a maximum of approximately 2 billion characters to a string variable.
- **Object.** A variable that contains a pointer to a defined object within VBA.
- **Variant.** A variable that can contain any type of data.

An additional data type (Decimal) is also specified in the VBA documentation, but is not currently supported by the language.

In order to make sure that your variable matches the type of data that you plan on storing in it, you should explicitly declare your variables near the beginning of your procedures. You do so by using the Dim keyword, in this manner:

```
Dim iMyInteger As Integer
```

The Dim keyword is followed by the name you want to use for the variable, the As keyword, and then the data type you want used for the variable. In this example, iMyInteger is the variable name. There is nothing special about this name, and I choose to put the "i" in front of it so that later I remember that the variable is an integer. I similarly preface other variable names with characters that indicate what data type I used for the variable.

Most of the VBA data types should be fairly self-explanatory, but there are a few that require special attention so you can understand them fully. These are examined in the following sections.

The Date Data Type

Dates and times are both stored in the Date data type using a serial number technique. The serial number consists of whole numbers (those to the left of the decimal point) that represent the number of days since January 1, 100 (yes, the year 100) and December 31, 9999. The portion to the right of the decimal point in the serial number represents the fraction of a day represented by the serial number.

The easiest way to set a Date variable is to use the following technique:

```
dMyDate = #6/15/2013#
```

When you enclose the date within two hash marks (number signs), VBA understands that it should be considered a date. You can also use two special VBA functions to assign dates, as shown here:

```
dMyDate = DateSerial(2013, 6, 15)
dMyDate = CDate("6/15/2013")
```

The first function (DateSerial) converts a year, month, and day into a date serial number. The second function (CDate) converts a text string into a date.

The Object Data Type

Objects are part and parcel of an object-oriented programming language such as Visual Basic for Applications; they are discussed more fully later in this chapter. They are used to access all the pieces and parts that Word is capable of working with in a document. The most likely time that you'll utilize objects is when you want to work with an object within Word's object model hierarchy.

The Variant Data Type

The Variant data type gets its name from its ability to vary its format, taking on the form of the data it contains. If you store a string in a variant, the variant appears as a String data type and can be manipulated by the String operators. If you store a number to a variant, it acts like a numeric variable and you can use the arithmetic operators in its manipulation.

While variants are convenient, in the sense that you don't have to think much to use them, I recommend that unless you have a specific need which can't be solved in any reasonable way without their use, you should avoid them. It's always better to have a thorough understanding of what your program is doing and why it is doing it. Using variants is like painting without first scraping, sanding, and priming. If everything under the new paint is OK you can get away without any extra work. If it's not, then the new paint is soon a mess and you are doing the job over.

Understanding Operators

Variables are the raw material of your programs. You work with that raw material using operators. Fortunately, VBA has a rich set of operators available. This operator set makes the job of programming much simpler.

As mentioned earlier in this chapter, variables are so named because their value can change—they can vary. This flexibility is the feature which makes them so useful. There are many ways to change the value contained in a variable.

When working with variables, the kind of manipulation you perform is defined by the operator. The operator is the symbol that defines what type of operation should take place in the equation. If there is only one variable being operated on, it is called the operand. If there is more than one variable, they are referred to collectively as the operands.

Arithmetic Operators

The most common category of operations involves arithmetic. You probably know most of the arithmetic operations, but VBA includes some useful ones you may not be familiar with. You probably already are familiar with + (addition), - (subtraction), * (multiplication), and / (division). Other arithmetic operators that may be more esoteric to you are ^ (exponentiation), \ (integer division), and Mod (modulus).

The exponentiation operator (the caret character, or **Shift+6** on the keyboard) is used to raise a number to a power. For instance, 2*2 is noted as 2^2 and 2*2*2 is noted as 2^3. You also can raise a number to a fractional exponent, as in 3 ^ 1.5. VBA also can do this, as well as handle numbers raised to negative exponents.

Integer division, represented by the backslash operator, takes two values as operands and returns an integer as the result. If you use a non-integer as one or both of the operands, the non-integer is converted to an integer first and then the division is performed. The result is always an integer. Be careful not to confuse integer division with normal division, which is represented by a forward slash. Each type of division produces different results.

The modulus operator (Mod) hearkens back to the days when you were first learning to divide. The answers you got to a problem such as "six divided by five" were "one remainder one". The remainder is what is left over after the division. The Mod operator returns the remainder of a division operation. Just like with the integer division operator, the operands are rounded to integers prior to the Mod operation being performed. Also, as with integer division, the result is always an integer.

Comparison Operators

The comparison operators are used when you want to know the magnitude of one variable compared to another. "Does variable1 contain a value which is larger, smaller, or exactly equal to variable2?" is the kind of question to which a comparison operator provides an answer.

The result of any comparison can only be True or False. In addition, comparison operators can be used on either numeric values or text values. The six comparison operators are as follows:

- = (equal)
- < (less than)
- > (greater than)
- <= (less than or equal)
- >= (greater than or equal)
- <> (not equal)

The equal operator is fairly straightforward. Just remember that equal means exactly equal. If two values differ by even the slightest amount, they are not evaluated as equal. The two values 4.0 and 4.0000000001 may look the same when displayed by your VBA programming (due to formatting), but the values in memory are different and therefore not equal.

When using the Greater Than and Less Than operators remember that any negative number is less than any positive number. This is easy to remember if you picture all numbers placed on a number line, like you used to use in elementary school. The line has 0 in the middle, the positive numbers (1,2,3, and so on) to the right, and the negative numbers (-1, -2, -3, and so on) heading off to the left. Pick any two numbers on this number line. The one on the left is always less and the one to the right is always more.

The Not Equal operator tells you if any two variables are different, even by the slightest amount. Not Equal can be used to determine if two dates or times are the same, if two files have identical names, or if the length of two files differ. It can be used anywhere you need to know if there is the slightest difference.

Less Than or Equal combines two questions into one. "Is value1 less than value2" OR "is value1 equal to value2". OR is shown in capitals to emphasize that if either of the conditions is met, the statement is True. Greater Than or Equal works in a similar (but opposite) manner.

Logical Operators

You use logical operators to build more complex logical constructs. For example, if you have a group of individuals and you want to locate all single red-headed males who are between the ages of 20 and 30 and who don't have a pet, logical operators provide the means. The following demonstrates:

```
(Married = "S") And (Hair = "Red") And (Age >= 20) And (Age <= 30) And (Pet = "None")
```

Logical operators allow you to apply Boolean logic to your data, determining a final solution that is either True or False. VBA provides the following logical operators:

- And
- Or
- Xor (exclusive Or)
- Eqv (equivalent)
- Imp (implication)
- Not (or the logical opposite of)

Normally VBA's logical operators are used in some sort of logical construct, such as an If … Then construct. A full discussion of these constructs is provided in Chapter 7, but a quick overview is provided in the examples here.

The And operator returns a True value only if both operands are True, otherwise the result if False. Here is an example of using the operator:

```
If (FirstName = "Tony") And (LastName = "Carpenter") Then
    MsgBox "Found Tony"
Else
    MsgBox "Tony could not be found!"
End If
```

Notice the use of parentheses in the example. Operations within parentheses are performed first and then the results are used in further calculations. This ensures that operations are performed in the order you intend. In the example above, FirstName is compared with "Tony" and LastName is compared with "Carpenter", then the results are compared.

The Or operator returns a True value if either of the operands are True. It only returns a False value if both of the operands are False:

```
If FirstName = "Beth" OR FirstName = "Ginger" Then
    MsgBox "Female"
End If
```

The Xor operator returns a True value when only one of the operands is True. It returns a False value whenever both operands are the same, whether they are both True or both False. Here is an example:

```
If (FirstName = "Tony") XOR (LastName = "Carpenter") Then
    MsgBox "Same first name or same last name but not both."
Else
    MsgBox "None with just the same first or last name."
End If
```

The Eqv operator returns a True value only if both operands are equal, otherwise the result is False. Here is an example:

```
If FirstName Eqv LastName Then
    DoError           'Signify error condition
End If
```

In all numeric situations the EQV operator is the same as using an equal sign in a comparison. Eqv does not act as a comparison operator for strings, however.

The Imp operator is the local implication operator. It returns a False value only if the second operand is False and the first is True, otherwise the result is True:

```
If (Price > 100000) Imp (Pay > 60000) Then
    MsgBox "Applicant doesn't qualify"      'Pay not high enough
Else
    MsgBox "Applicant appears to qualify"
End If
```

The Not operator differs from the other logical operators in that it does not require two operands. Instead, it performs a logical negation of a value. In other words, a True value is changed to False and vice versa. The following is an example of how you could use the NOT operator in an equation.

```
If Not (PayLevel > 1000) Then
    MsgBox "Pay is very low for this job."
End If
```

String Operators

Earlier you learned about comparison operators and how they can be used to compare numeric values. Comparison operators also can be used with strings, and then the result used in further computations. In addition, VBA provides a way to concatenate (combine) strings together. Consider the following code fragment:

```
sFirstName = "John"
sLastName = "Davis"
sFullName = sFirstName & " " & sLastName
sSortName = sLastName & ", " & sFirstName
```

When this code is executed, the sFullName variable contains the characters "John Davis" and the sSortName variable contains "Davis, John".

You'll find that strings and string operations are involved in virtually every program you can imagine.

Using Objects and Collections

As mentioned earlier, Visual Basic for Applications is an object-oriented programming language. This means that it works with objects and collections of objects. This may sound a bit odd, but it is no different than us as humans—we work with objects, as well.

Consider your home for a moment; it contains many objects and collections of objects. For instance, if you walk into your kitchen you may find a dish on the counter. This dish is a single object, but it is also a member of a larger collection of objects referred to as dishes. You can do things with the single dish (just like VBA can do things with a single object) or you or you can do things with the entire collection of dishes (just like VBA can do things with a collection of objects).

In the following section you get a quick introduction to the way that VBA works with Word's available objects and object collections.

Word's Object Model

You may consider it a rather obvious statement to say that Word allows you to work with documents. It is, after all, a word processor. While you may intuitively understand what a document is, VBA does not; remember that it can only do work with objects. Fortunately, Word makes certain objects accessible to VBA and allows them to be worked with. Documents are an example of the type of objects that Word makes available to VBA.

In fact, there are many, many different types of objects that Word makes available. All of these objects, taken together, are referred to as Word's *object model*. If you understand just a bit about this model, then you'll start to understand how you can access, modify, and otherwise use the various objects available to Word and to VBA.

There are literally hundreds of different objects that Word allows you to access through VBA. To get an idea of what objects are available, take a look at Word's help system for VBA. Follow these steps if you are using Word 2007 or Word 2010:

1. Display the Visual Basic Editor. (The easiest way is to simply press ALT+F11 while in Word.)
2. With the Visual Basic Editor visible, press F1. Word displays the help system for VBA.
3. On the main screen for the help system, click the Word Object Model Reference link. What you see should be similar to what is shown in Figure 2-2.

If you are using Word 2013 then finding the right information involves a few more steps:

1. Display the Visual Basic Editor. (The easiest way is to simply press ALT+F11 while in Word.)
2. With the Visual Basic Editor visible, press F1. Word displays the help system for VBA, which is actually the MSDN Library. (You may see some help information displayed, depending on what was selected in the Visual Basic Editor when you pressed F1. You can safely ignore what you see in this regard.)

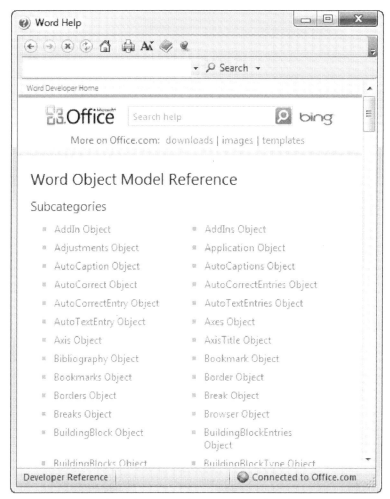

Figure 2-2. *The help system for VBA provides documentation for all of the objects in Word's object model.*

3. In the MSDN Library hierarchy, at the left side of the screen, lick Office and SharePoint Development. You'll see a number of options appear under that option.

4. Click Office Client Development. More options appear.

5. Click Office 2013. Again, more options appear. (If you can't tell, you are "drilling down" through the options in the MSDN Library hierarchy.)

6. Click Word 2013. Still more options appear.

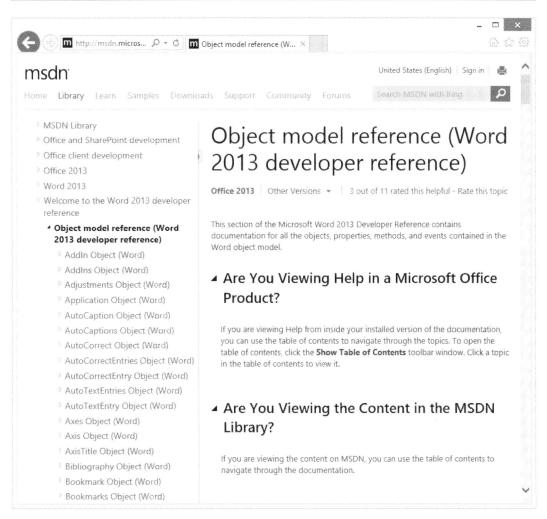

Figure 2-3. *The MSDN Library help system for VBA in Word 2013 can also provide documentation for all of the objects in Word's object model.*

7. Click Welcome to the Word 2013 Developer Reference. Even more options appear.
8. Click Object Model Reference. Your screen should now be similar to what you seen in Figure 2-3.

The topics listed in the Subcategories section (Word 2007 or Word 2010) or in the MSDN Library hierarchy (Word 2013) represent the various objects available in Word. Scroll through them; you'll discover hundreds of different objects. You can figure out the purpose of most of the objects just by looking at their names. For instance, you can probably figure out that the Shape object represents a graphic shape that you add to your document.

Take some time to look through the list of objects available in Word, but don't let the sheer number of objects overwhelm you. As you work in the Visual Basic Editor, you'll find that it is quite helpful on suggesting the names of objects that you may want to work with. (This becomes apparent as you start to type VBA statements into the editor.)

In reality, you'll find that you only work with a handful of different objects. These are the objects that you'll probably work with the most:

- **Application.** This object is the top-level object in Word. It is called the Application object because it represents the currently running version of Word. Every other object belongs to the Application object.
- **Document.** You can probably figure out that a Document object represents a single Word document. This is a document that is open within the program; it is not an unopened document on your hard drive. Document objects belong to the Application object and they can contain many other types of objects.
- **Range.** This is a very common object that belongs to many higher-level objects. It represents the entirety of whatever object to which it belongs and it functions as a "gateway" that allows you to access various elements of the higher-level object.
- **Selection.** This object represents whatever is selected within the document at the time that the macro is running.

Grouping Similar Objects Together

Word automatically groups similar objects together into what are called *collections*. For instance, individual Document objects are grouped together in the Documents collection and individual Shape objects are grouped in the Shapes collection.

If you examine objects in Word's object model (see Figure 2-2), take note of the plural object names: AddIns, AutoCorrectEntries, AutoTextEntries, Axes, Bookmarks, Borders, etc. Each of these is a collection of individual objects. VBA allows you to access individual members of collections or to work with an entire collection.

Assigning Objects to Variables

Earlier in this chapter you learned about how VBA works with variables. When you are working with the various objects in Word's object model, you'll often find it helpful to assign an object to a variable. This makes it easier in the program to later work with the various members of the object. (Object members are described in the next section.)

To assign an object to a variable, you use the Set keyword. For example, you might want to work with the first paragraph of a document. You can define the variable you are going to use for this purpose in this manner:

```
Dim rFirstPar As Range
```

When you later want to assign the actual object for the paragraph to the variable, you do so with this statement:

```
Set rFirstPar = Documents(1).Paragraphs(1).Range
```

This assigns the Range object of the Paragraphs(1) object of the Documents(1) object to the rFirstPar variable. (That's a mouthful, huh?) This variable now contains the Range object and you can access that object using the variable at any time. Essentially, the rFirstPar variable contains the first paragraph of the document.

If you later no longer need to reference the rFirstPar object, you can use the Set keyword to get rid of the variable in this manner:

```
Set rFirstPar = Nothing
```

Understanding Object Members

Objects or collections of objects can have a number of different members that belong to them. These members are of two primary types: methods and properties. It is important to understand more about these members, as they represent the "meat and bones" of working with objects.

Doing Operations with Methods

The easiest way to look at a method is as some sort of process that Word allows you to perform using an object. For instance, you might want your macro to create a new document. You do this by using the Add method for the Documents collection, in this manner:

```
Documents.Add
```

Note that you separate the object name (in this case Documents) from the method name (Add) by a single period. When this line is executed, VBA dutifully adds a new, empty document to the collection of open documents. The period is used to specify a movement down a level in the hierarchy of Word's object model. As you move from left to right on the line, each period you encounter represents another movement through the hierarchy.

The number and type of methods available for an object depends on the nature of the object to which the methods belong. For instance, the Hyperlink object possesses a Follow method that is used to display the target of that hyperlink. It doesn't make sense that the Follow method would be available with other objects, such as a Document or a Bookmark.

Working with Properties

Each object in the Word object model possesses a group of *properties*. These are nothing but attributes or characteristics that belong to or describe the object. For instance, in real life if you are looking at a dish in your kitchen, its characteristics might be its diameter, its depth, its color, or any number of other descriptors. These are, in the object-oriented world, properties of the object.

As an example, the Envelope object has a good number of properties, such as Address, AddressFromLef, AddressFromTop, ReturnAddress, and many more. In total, there are almost 30 different properties associated with the Envelope object. They describe characteristics of the envelope, in exquisite detail.

When creating programming statements in VBA, you refer to properties using the same technique that you refer to methods. For instance, suppose you wanted to assign the text of a document's first paragraph to a string variable:

```
sRawText = Documents(1).Paragraphs(1).Range.Text
```

After this statement is executed, the sRawText variable contains all the text that was in the document's first paragraph. As described earlier in the chapter, you can assign an object (such as the first paragraph of a document) to a variable and then later use that variable to reference the properties of the object represented by the variable, in this manner:

```
Set rFirstPar = Documents(1).Paragraphs(1).Range
sRawText = rFirstPar.Text
```

An important concept about properties is that some of them can be written to (you can change them) and some properties can only be read. You'll discover which properties are of which type by trial and error and by examining the online documentation for each property.

Finally, it is important to understand that some properties are fully objects in their own right. Consider the following programming statement:

```
sParStyle = Documents(1).Paragraphs(12).Style
```

This line sets the sParStyle variable equal to the name of the style for the twelfth paragraph in the document. In this instance, the primary object is Documents(1), which is the first document in the documents collection. Everything after that point is considered a property of that primary object. Thus, Paragraphs(12) is a property of the primary object, even though it is an object in its own right. The Style property is simply that—a property of the object/property that precedes it in the hierarchy.

Making Sense of Members

Since there are hundreds of different objects available in the Word object model, there are thousands of different methods provided to work with those objects and even more properties for those objects. It is impossible for a human to keep track of that number of methods and properties, so it is fortunate that the Visual Basic Editor provides some help for you, automatically.

Remember that it was noted earlier that periods are used to denote movement through Word's object model hierarchy. Thus, the following statement, which uses two periods, denotes the movement through several layers of the hierarchy:

```
Set rFirstPar = Documents(1).Paragraphs(1).Range
```

As you start typing a statement such as this into the Visual Basic Editor, every time you type a period you'll see a list of options based upon the level of the hierarchy you are currently traversing. The options are shown in a drop-down list of members, with an indicator as to whether the member is a method or property, as shown here:

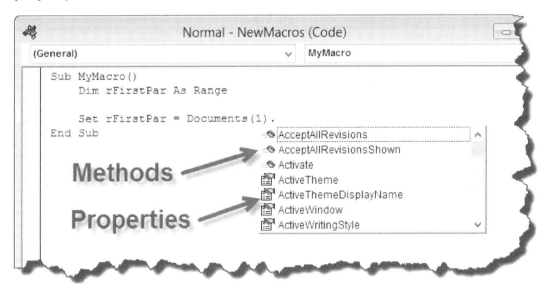

Note that the drop-down list of members is dynamic; it always changes depending on what is possible to come next, based upon the hierarchy of Word's object model.

40

VBA Constants

Besides variables (which you already learned about), VBA also allows you to work with constants. Remember that variables are called such because they can vary. Similarly, constants are called such because they remain constant; they don't vary. In VBA constants are of three types: literal, symbolic, or enums.

Using Literal Constants

Literal constants are very simple in nature. You can use them on the right side of most any operator. The following is, perhaps, the simplest example possible of using literal constants:

```
X = 2 + 3
```

Obviously this formula ends up in the variable X being equal to 5, but it is not X on which you should focus. Both 2 and 3 are constants—they don't change. Constants can also be text strings, in which case they are surrounded by quote marks:

```
sMyString = "abc" & " " & "def"
```

In this instance there are three constants, each surrounded by quote marks that are concatenated together and assigned to the sMyString variable.

Finally, you can also enclose date and time constants with hash marks or number signs:

```
dMyDate = #6/11/2000#
```

Creating Symbolic Constants

Symbolic constants are similar to variables in that they are declared within a program and given a name (a symbolic name, if you prefer) that can subsequently be used in the program. Consider the following example:

```
Const sMyName = "Allen Wyatt"
```

The Const keyword tells VBA that you are setting up a constant. It is followed by the name you want used for this constant (sMyName), the equal sign, and the value you want used for the constant. If you later use the name sMyName in your coding, then VBA knows that you really mean "Allen Wyatt".

As mentioned earlier, the values of constants cannot change within your program once they are set. If you try to change the value of a constant, VBA generates an error. For instance, if your program included the constant declaration above, then the following line elsewhere in your program would generate an error:

```
sMyName = "Somebody else"
```

Word's Enumerations

The third type of constant is more correctly known as an *enumeration*, or enum for short. Don't let the fancy name fool you; these are nothing but system-defined symbolic constants. VBA provides a wide variety of enums (somewhere in excess of 700 of them) that are used for a wide variety of things. For instance, the enum vbCrLf is a constant for the ASCII codes for a carriage return and a line feed:

```
MsgBox "You made a mistake" & vbCrLf & "Try again"
```

VBA enums always start with the lowercase letters *vb* (as in vbCrLf or vbTab). If you see some enums that start with the lowercase letters *wd* (as in wdAlignParagraphLeft or wdColorDarkBlue), that means that the enum is a part of the Word's object model. Word provides somewhere around 2,000 different enumeration constants for its object model.

3

Naming Considerations

One of the first tasks you need to figure out how to do when working with macros is to figure out what to name them. It isn't as trivial of a task as it may seem, however. Names of macros are very important, and this chapter is designed to help you understand all the ins and outs of the names you may consider.

In this chapter you discover the following:

- How to create your own macro names
- How to rename an existing macro
- Where your macros are stored
- Understanding event handlers
- Word's special automatic macros
- How to change Word's built-in commands

Naming Macros

Whenever you choose to create a macro (see Chapter 2) you'll need to come up with a name for that macro. VBA is fairly flexible in allowing you to name your macros. In fact, there are only three simple rules you need to follow:

- Your macro names must start with a letter, after which they can contain letters, numbers, and underscores.

- Your macro names must not contain any spaces, symbols (except the underscore), or punctuation marks.
- Macro names must not be longer than 80 characters.

If you try to use a macro name that violates these three rules, you'll see an error message displayed and have the opportunity to correct your violation. In order to make sure your macros are as usable as possible, you'll want to make sure that the name you use is clear, descriptive, and only as long as it needs to be to avoid confusion.

It is also a good idea to not use a macro name that matches any existing VBA function or enum. (Functions are discussed in Chapter 6 and enumerations are introduced at the end of Chapter 2.) If you do so the results may be unpredictable.

One good idea is to make sure that your macros all start with some unique letter sequence that makes sense for your system. For instance, you may want to start all your macros with your three initials. Doing so allows you to easily differentiate those macros you created from any other macros that may be on your system. Plus, it is unlikely that your initials conflict with the start of any of Word's or VBA's built-in features.

Renaming Macros

At its heart a macro is nothing more than a series of instructions you want the computer to execute. It is a program that is run in the framework provided by Microsoft Word. As you create macros, you'll probably come across a need to rename a few of the macros you previously created. To do this it's easiest to work with the Visual Basic Editor. Follow these steps:

1. Press **ALT+F11**. Word displays the Visual Basic Editor.
2. In the Code window, use the Procedure drop-down list to choose the procedure you want to rename. The procedure you select is displayed in the window.
3. At the top of the macro you'll see the procedure definition, consisting of the word "Sub" or Function followed by the name of the macro.

Chapter 3: Naming Considerations

Change the actual name in this line. (Don't change the keywords Sub or Function or the space that follows the keywords Sub or function, and don't change anything starting with the left parenthesis that follows the name of the procedure.)

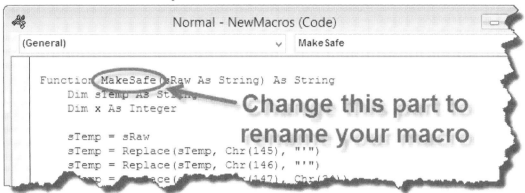

4. Close the Visual Basic Editor.

That's it; the macro is now renamed to whatever name you used in step 3.

If you change the name of a function that you previously created, you'll also want to search through the rest of your project and see if your function is called from any of your other code. Changing the name of the function by following the above steps doesn't change any code that calls the old name; you need to do that manually. If you don't make these changes, then you'll get an error whenever you try to run a macro that references the old function name.

Where Macros are Stored

You know where Word stores your documents—on your hard drive or on some other storage medium, such as a thumb drive. Macros, though, aren't stored in dedicated files in this manner. Instead, macros are stored as part of other files, much like graphics or text boxes are stored as part of a different file (document files).

Early in Chapter 2 you learned about modules and how VBA procedures are stored in those modules. You can store VBA modules with any type of Word document, whether it is a regular document or a template. In fact, when you save a document or template, Word changes the filename extension based on whether there is a VBA module in the file:

- **DOCX.** This is a regular Word document that doesn't contain any macros.
- **DOCM.** This is a regular Word document that contains at least one VBA module.
- **DOTX.** This is a Word template that doesn't contain any macros.
- **DOTM.** This is a Word template that contains at least one VBA module.

By default Word stores your macros as part of the Normal.dotm template—the Normal template available to all Word documents, but enabled for macro modules. In order to store your macros in a different place you'll need to specify that other place when creating the macro. How you do that depends on whether you are recording a macro or creating one from scratch.

Specifying a Location when Recording a Macro

In Chapter 1 you discovered how easy it is to record a series of actions as a macro. What you may not have realized was that as part of the recording process Word gives you the chance to specify where you want to save the macro you are recording. To see where this occurs, start by displaying the Developer tab of the ribbon. Then click the Record Macro tool in the Code group. Word displays the Record Macro dialog box, shown in Figure 3-1.

Note that the dialog box includes a drop-down list called Store Macro In. If you click this list, Word provides a number of options for you. The top option is always All Document (Normal.dotm). This is the default choice; it means that the macro is stored in the Normal.dotm template and is therefore available regardless of which document is open on your screen.

The other options available in the drop-down list depend on how you are using Word at the moment. Basically you'll see an option in the list for each document open in Word and each template open in Word. Note that Word even provides options for all the non-macro-enabled documents and templates; those that end with the DOCX or DOTX filename extensions. If you choose one of these as the place where your macro should be stored, then the next time you chose

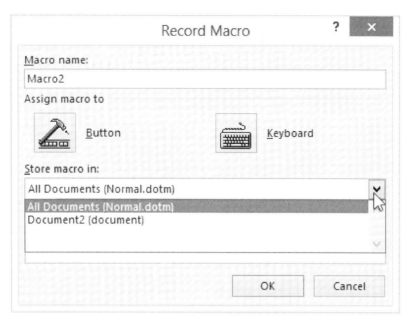

Figure 3-1. When recording a macro you can specify where the macro is to be stored by using the Store Macro In drop-down list.

to save that document or template, Word asks you to save it using the DOCM or DOTM extensions.

Specifying a Location when Creating a Macro from Scratch

Choosing where Word stores your from-scratch macros is similar to choosing where it saves your recorded macros. The biggest difference is that you make the selection in the Macro dialog box instead of the in the Record Macro dialog box. The easiest way to display this dialog box is to simply press ALT+**F8**. You can then click the Macros In drop-down list to see places where macros can be stored (see Figure 3-2).

If you compare Figure 3-2 with what is shown in Figure 3-1, you can probably figure out how the various options correlate with each other. It is interesting to note that that wording of the available options is different, even though they do the same things. Basically the meaningful options are as follows:

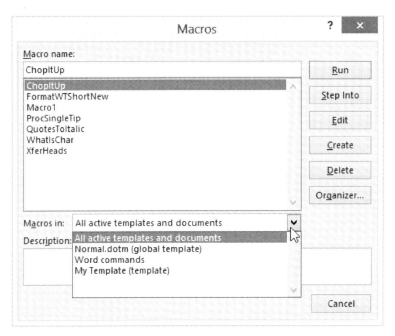

Figure 3-2. *When creating macro from scratch you can specify where the macro is to be stored by using the Macros In drop-down list.*

- **Normal.dotm.** This is the Normal template and is available to all documents at all times in Word.
- **Word commands.** This is the list of built-in Word functions. You can't actually store your macros here; the option is available in expectation that you might want to change an existing Word command, as described later in this chapter.
- **Templates.** Each of your currently open templates is available in the drop-down list.
- **Documents.** Each of your currently open documents is available in the drop-down list.

Choose where you want your macro stored, and once you click on Create then Word opens the Code window for the appropriate module in that template or document.

Event Handlers

Objects within Word can have events handlers associated with them. An event handler is a special type of macro that is triggered (executed) whenever a particular event occurs. Most event handlers are associated with the special ThisDocument object, which exists for every document you create in Word.

To see what events are available, follow these steps:

1. Press **ALT+F11** to display the Visual Basic Editor.
2. Note the Project Explorer window, at the left side of the editor. (The Project Explorer is explained in more detail in Chapter 4.) If the Project Explorer window is not visible for some reason, press **CTRL+R** to display it.
3. Note that the Project Explorer shows each open document as a separate project. Locate the document (project) for which you want to create an event handler.
4. Double-click the ThisDocument object, in the Project Explorer, for the document you located. (See Figure 3-3.) A code window for the document is opened.
5. Click the Procedure down-arrow (see Figure 3-4) to see the events that can be handled for the document.

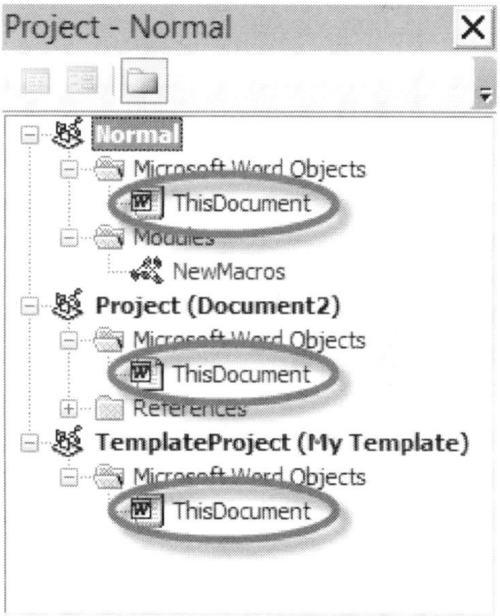

Figure 3-3. Double-clicking the ThisDocument object opens a code window for that object.

Note in Figure 3-4 that Word created, automatically, an event handler named Document_New. There are several other events that are available in the drop-down list, as follows:

- **Document_BuildingBlockInsert.** This event is triggered whenever an existing building block is inserted in the document.

Figure 3-4. *Clicking the Procedure down-arrow shows a list of events available for the ThisDocument object.*

- **Document_Close.** This event is triggered whenever this particular document is closed.
- **Document_ContentControlAfterAdd.** This event is triggered when a content control is added to the document.
- **Document_ContentControlBeforeContentUpdate.** This event is triggered before updating the content in a content control, but only when the content comes from the Office XML data store.
- **Document_ContentControlBeforeDelete.** This event is triggered before a content control is deleted from the document.

- **Document_ContentControlBeforeStoreUpdate.** This event is triggered before the document's XML data store is updated with the value of a content control.

- **Document_ContentControlOnEnter.** This event is triggered whenever the user enters (selects) a content control.

- **Document_ContentControlOnExit.** This event is triggered whenever the user exits a content control by moving to a different content control or by moving to some other area of the document.

- **Document_New.** This event is triggered whenever this particular document is open and you then create a new document. This event is particularly helpful if it is associated with a template, as it is triggered whenever you create a new document based on the template.

- **Document_Open.** This event is triggered whenever the document is first opened.

- **Document_Sync.** This event is triggered when the document is synchronized with a copy of the document that resides on a document server.

- **Document_XMLAfterInsert.** This event is triggered when each new XML element is added to the document.

- **Document_XMLBeforeDelete.** This event is triggered before each existing XML element is deleted from the document.

Most of the events for which you can create handlers are pretty advanced, having to do with things like remote servers, XML, and XML stores. In all likelihood, the only events for which you might create handlers are the Document_Close, Document_New, and Document_Open events. In the next section you'll learn of alternative ways to run a macro when any of these three events occur.

Automatic Macros

Besides the event handlers described in the previous section, Word includes a few names for macros that it considers special. These special names, when given to your macros, perform tasks without any intervention on your part. For instance, you can create a macro that Word runs automatically whenever you create a document.

These special macros that automatically run at predefined times are identified by special names. Otherwise, there is nothing different between these macros and any other you may write. Here are the names you can give macros so that they run automatically.

- **AutoOpen.** A macro that possesses this name is run whenever you open a document.
- **AutoClose.** A macro using this name is run whenever you close a document.
- **AutoNew.** A macro saved under this name is automatically run whenever you create a new document.
- **AutoExec.** A macro that uses this name is run whenever you start Word.
- **AutoExit.** This name for a macro means that it is run whenever you exit Word.

Why would you want to use these automatic macros? You might have some special tasks that need to be completed relative to a specific document. In this case, you'll want to make sure that you save the automatic macro with the document itself, instead of with a template or in Normal.dotm.

For example, let's say that you have an important document and when it is opened by someone you want to remind the user to save the document regularly. An easy way to do that is to simply create an AutoOpen macro and save it in the important document. It could be very simple, like this:

```
Sub AutoOpen()
    sTemp = "This is an important document." & vbCrLf
    sTemp = sTemp & "Please make sure you save this document" & vbCrLf
    sTemp = sTemp & "every few minutes while you are editing."
    MsgBox sTemp
End Sub
```

Once you save the macro with the document (remember you'll need to save the document as a macro-enabled document) then the macro is in place. The next time the document is opened the user is shown a message box with your request. (Message boxes are discussed in detail in Chapter 9.)

Changing Built-In Word Commands

Word allows you not only to edit macros, but also to edit built-in commands. Word includes literally hundreds of built-in commands, many of which are executed whenever you use the various tools available on the ribbon tabs. You can replace or augment these commands with your own macros. You perform the editing by following these steps:

1. Press **ALT+F8**. Word displays the Macros dialog box.
2. Using the Macros In drop-down list, select Word Commands. (See Figure 3-5.)
3. Using the command list, locate and select the command you want to edit. Once selected, the name should appear not only in the list of commands, but also in the Macro Name box at the top of the dialog box.

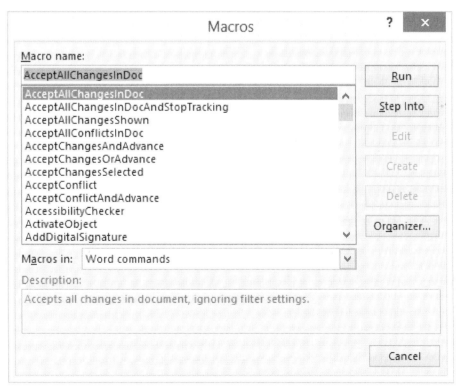

Figure 3-5. Word allows you to modify the program's built-in commands using the Visual Basic Editor.

4. Using the Macros In drop-down list, select where you want your edited command to appear. For instance, you could select All Active Templates and Documents, or you could select a specific template or document name where your new command should be stored. The command name should still appear in the Macro Name box at the top of the dialog box.

5. Click on Create. (The Create button is not clickable until you perform step 4.) Word starts the Visual Basic Editor and shows the program instructions that make up the built-in command.

6. Make your changes to the command.

Note in step 5 that the program instructions that make up the built-in command are provided as a starting point for your editing. Any changes you make to the command are used, by Word, in preference to the regular instructions for the command. For instance, the following is the code displayed in the Visual Basic Editor if you choose (in step 3) to edit the FileSave command:

```
Sub FileSave()
'
' FileSave Macro
' Saves the active document or template
'
    ActiveDocument.Save

End Sub
```

The macro consists of a single command line that saves the document. You may want to modify the code so that the document is saved in a particular location or so it is saved in multiple locations or so it is saved using some name you specify. The ways in which you can modify the command are, literally, endless.

Remember that the key to Word using your macro instructions in preference to the built-in command is the name of the macro. If you change the macro name from the name that Word uses for the built-in command, then your macro won't be automatically run when the built-in command is executed.

A modified Word command is only in effect for the document in which you save the command or, if you save it in a template, if the template is associated with the document on which you are working. To get rid of your modified command, all you need to do is delete it fully in the Visual Basic Editor.

Understanding the VBA Environment

Visual Basic for Applications offers a simple approach to programming macros that work within the framework offered by Word. With VBA you can quickly and easily create macros that automate common tasks and make processing your documents a snap.

In this chapter you discover more about the environment in which VBA macros are run. Specifically, you learn how to use the Visual Basic Editor and everything that it offers. By the end of the chapter you'll have the following under your belt:

- How to display the Visual Basic Editor
- All the pieces and parts of the editor environment
- How to get help in the editor
- Ways you can customize how the editor does its work
- Exiting the Visual Basic Editor

Displaying the Visual Basic Editor

You've probably gotten the idea by now that the Visual Basic Editor is intrinsic to working with Word macros. (If you haven't gotten that idea, now would be a good time to get it.) Regardless of whether you record macros and later edit them or simply create your macros from scratch, working with the Visual Basic Editor is critical.

There are a few ways you can display the Visual Basic Editor. Any of these methods work:

- Display the Developer tab of the ribbon and click the Visual Basic tool in the Code group.
- Press **Alt+F11**.
- Display the Macros dialog box and use either the Edit or Create buttons.

Regardless of how you start the Visual Basic Editor, you'll soon see a screen similar to what you see in Figure 4-1.

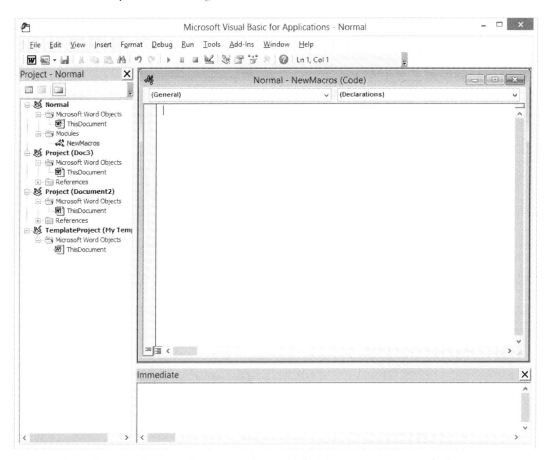

Figure 4-1. The Visual Basic Editor is used to modify the programming code for your macros.

Chapter 4: Understanding the VBA Environment

The Visual Basic Editor uses the older, menu-based interface familiar to long-time Word users. Don't worry if what you see in the Visual Basic Editor is a bit different than what you see in Figure 4-1; it is possible for some of the elements of the interface to be turned off or obscured by some other part.

Parts of the Environment

Throughout the earlier parts of this book I've essentially taken the Visual Basic Editor for granted, having you display it to accomplish some rudimentary tasks, but I never took the time to explain the different parts of the editor. Each part of the editor performs a valuable function, so you'll benefit by knowing more about them. The following sections examine each of those parts.

The Menu Bar

In order to get things done in the Visual Basic Editor, you need to learn how to use the menu bar. The menu bar contains the major categories of tasks you may want to accomplish with the editor. It is located just under the Visual Basic Editor's title bar:

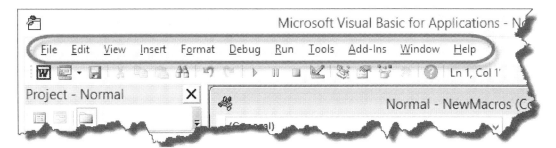

You can select menus with either the mouse or the keyboard. To select a menu with the mouse, just point to the menu name and click the left button. A pull-down menu appears. Using the keyboard, however, requires a little more information.

Notice that the first character of each menu name in the menu bar is underlined. The underlined character is the access key for that menu. In some other programs, these access keys are often called *hot keys*. To activate a menu, press and hold the ALT key and then press the relative access key. For example, to pull down the File menu, press and hold the ALT key and then press F.

After you pull down a menu, notice that each menu item also has an access key. Unlike the menu names, the access key for a menu item isn't always the first letter. This is because many menu items start with the same letters. If the first letter was always underlined, then the access keys wouldn't be unique. The access key would still work—Word would simply cycle through all the menu items using that particular access key, highlighting each of them in turn. To execute a particular item, you would have to press the ENTER key. For rapid access, reduced confusion, and ease of use, other letters in the menu item are defined as the access key instead. The underlined letter within a menu item is always the access key for that menu item.

Selecting a menu item using an access key is even easier than selecting a menu. Just press the access key without pressing the ALT key. For example, to select the Save menu item, while the File menu is open, press S without using ALT. What could be faster? Shortcut keys!

As their name implies, shortcut keys provide an even faster way of selecting menu items. Pull down the File menu again:

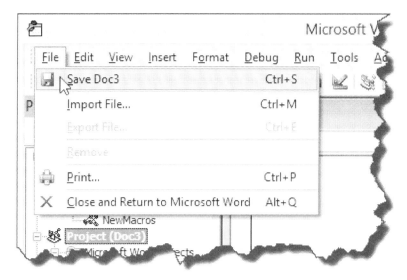

Notice the five menu items that have additional text on the right side of the menu list. For example, the Print menu item has CTRL+P next to it. This text represents the shortcut keystroke to access that menu item directly, without having to pull down the File menu and then select Print. The plus sign (+) between the two keys signifies that the first key should be pressed and held while the second key is pressed.

Try to access the same menu item using each technique. First use the access keys to select Print from the File menu. The Print dialog box appears. Then select the Cancel button to close the dialog box without taking any action. Now try the shortcut key. Without any menus pulled down, press and hold the **CTRL** key and then press the **P** key. The Print dialog box appears immediately.

While some shortcut keys are assigned for compatibility with other Windows programs (such as **CTRL+P**), the rest are assigned based on frequency of use. The operations performed most frequently are assigned to function keys. These are the special keys across the top or on the left side of your keyboard; each one begins with the letter F, as in **F1**, **F2**, **F3**, and so on. Operations assigned to function keys are handy because they only require a single key press. You'll appreciate this feature while you are getting started with the Visual Basic Editor. As an example, the very first function key, **F1**, instantly invokes the on-line help.

Some menu items are executed immediately while others require more information. A menu item followed by ellipsis points (…) indicates that choosing the item does not execute the command immediately. You'll either see another menu or a dialog box. You saw this earlier when you accessed the Print dialog box using File | Print.

While you are using the Visual Basic Editor, not all menu items are applicable at all times. When you can't use a menu item, it is grayed. Menu items normally appear as black text. When the text is gray you can still see the item, but you can't select it. Items are grayed rather than removed so you can remember menu item locations.

The Toolbar

The Toolbar is the row of picture buttons under the menu bar. The icons on the face of the buttons represent the action taken when you press that button. Each Toolbar button represents a frequently performed action.

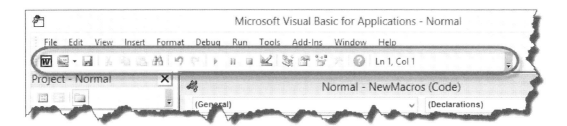

Using the Toolbar buttons makes performing actions faster and easier. Don't worry if you can't remember what each button does; there are menu items that perform the same operation as each Toolbar button. You can also get a hint as to what each Toolbar button does by hovering the mouse pointer over the button in question. After a second or two Word displays a ToolTip that provides additional information.

If you look closely at the Toolbar, you may notice that some of the buttons lack color. For instance, in the above image of the Toolbar the fourth and fifth buttons from the left lack color. (These are the buttons that look like a pair of scissors and two sheets of paper. They represent the Cut and Copy commands, respectively.) If you see buttons that lack color, it means that they are "greyed out" and not accessible at the moment. Word tries its best to make sure that only those tools that make sense at the moment are accessible.

You may find that you don't use the Toolbar and would prefer the additional screen space for other purposes. You can hide the Toolbar by selecting View | Toolbars | Standard. Notice that when the Toolbar is visible a check mark appears to the left of the menu item and when the Toolbar isn't visible there is no check mark. This is the editor's way of telling you whether the Toolbar is on or off.

The Project Explorer

VBA relies upon the concept of working with projects. Essentially, each document or template that is open in Word is considered a project. These projects serve as "containers" (for lack of a better word) for groups of objects. In VBA these objects are things like code modules, forms, and references to objects in other projects. The different things that can be stored in a project are discussed in Chapter 2.

Chapter 4: Understanding the VBA Environment

Helping you to keep track of the different projects open at any given time is the purpose of the Project Explorer. This window is visible, by default, at the left side of the Visual Basic Editor. If, for some reason, the Project Explorer is not visible on your system, you can display it by choosing View | Project Explorer or by pressing CTRL+R.

The Project Explorer is displayed in a hierarchical format. Notice that it contains textual descriptions of the various projects and their pieces, as well as a plus or minus sign to the left side of any item. The plus and minus signs are used to expand or contract each item, either showing or hiding the item's details.

The Properties Window

Another important part of the VBA environment is the Properties window. This window isn't shown by default, but it is easily displayed by choosing View | Properties Window or by pressing F4. The Properties window is used to display the behind-the-scenes properties for whatever you've selected in the Project Explorer.

In many cases—particularly if you are creating simple macros—you really don't need to worry about displaying the Properties window. (This may actually be the reason that Microsoft chooses not to display the window by default.) The Properties window is most valuable when your project includes user forms or other objects whose characteristics you want to easily modify.

There is a reciprocal relationship between an object in your project and the information in the Properties window. The information in the window changes as you select different objects or as you use the mouse to change an object. Conversely, you can modify the information in the Properties window and your changes are automatically reflected in the object.

If you don't have a specific need for the Properties window, it is a good idea to keep it hidden. You'll find that you have more room for other elements of the Visual Basic Editor (most notably the Code window) if you don't display the Properties window.

The Code Window

The place where you do the majority of your work in the Visual Basic Editor is known as the Code window. Because of its importance, the Code window typically occupies the largest portion of the Visual Basic Editor. The Code window is shown in Figure 4-2.

The Code window includes four distinct controls around the edges of the window:

- **Object List.** If your code module contains multiple objects (which is typically not the case), then you can select which object you want to work on using this drop-down list. When working on simple macros, the default selection of General is more than adequate.
- **Procedure List.** This drop-down list is used to specify the name of the procedure in which the insertion point is located. Generally it can be thought of as the procedure on which you are currently working. If you

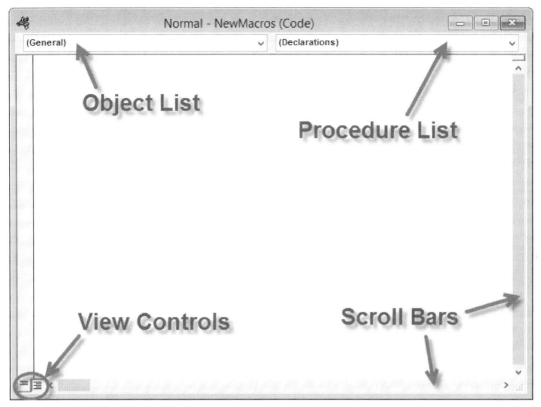

Figure 4-2. The Code window is where you do most of your work in the Visual Basic Editor.

use the drop-down list to select a procedure, the insertion point jumps to the beginning of whatever procedure you choose.

- **View Controls.** The two view controls in the lower-left corner of the Code window are used to specify what is displayed in the window. The leftmost button, when chosen, displays only whatever procedure you are working on. The rightmost button, which is the default, causes all the procedures in the current object to be listed at once.
- **Scroll Bars.** These function just the same as scroll bars do when working with a Word document. They allow you to scroll left or right (the horizontal scroll bar) or up and down (the vertical scroll bar).

The Visual Basic Editor allows you to have more than one Code window open at a time in the editor. This comes in handy when you need to copy some of your programming code from one module to another or when you need to see how you accomplished something in a different module than the one on which you are working.

The Immediate Window

Just under the Code window is the Immediate window. This window may not always be visible, but it is a good idea to have it displayed as you are working with your macro code. This is particularly true if you are trying to debug your code, as discussed in Chapter 15. If the Immediate window is not visible, you can display it by choosing View | Immediate Window or by pressing **Ctrl+G**.

The biggest use for the Immediate window is to try out some VBA statement or to see the value stored in a variable. I normally use the window while stepping through a macro. All I need to do is type, within the window, a question mark (which is VBA shorthand for "print") followed by a space and the name of the variable:

```
Immediate
? sTemp
Working throgh the document...
```

You can also use the same technique to display the results of VBA statements or functions:

```
Immediate
? len(sTemp)
 30
? 2 + 4
 6
```

Getting Help

The Visual Basic Editor comes with a complete on-line help system that is very useful as you learn to program. You access the on-line help system by any of the following means:

- Choose an option from the Help menu.
- Click the Help button on the Toolbar.
- Press the **F1** key.

When you choose the Help menu, another menu appears that lists the different types of help you can receive. These options are very similar to help options for other Windows programs; if you are comfortable with using the help system in other programs, you'll feel right at home here.

The other two ways to access the help system are essentially synonymous. The advantage of using either of these methods over using the menu is that they are context sensitive. This means that the Visual Basic Editor determines what you are currently doing and then displays the help information that it believes is the most appropriate to your needs.

For example, if you are typing a VBA statement in the Code window and you need assistance with a particular keyword, just make sure the insertion point is in the keyword and press **F1**. The help system springs into action and jumps directly to the information for that keyword. This method of accessing the help system also works for different elements of the VBA environment, such as the menu options, the Toolbar, and the Project Explorer. Just select the item that you need help with and then press **F1**. Figure 4-3 shows an example of the help screen displayed by Excel 2010 when you press **F1** after selecting the Project Explorer window.

Understand that exactly what you see when you press **F1** depends entirely on the version of Word you are using. Microsoft is notorious for making wholesale changes to the help system from version to version of the software.

Figure 4-3. The help system can provide context-sensitive help on a wide variety of topics.

Searching for Help

One of the most powerful features of the help system is the ability to search for topics on which you need more information. This is done in either of two ways:

- Display the help system window (an example is in Figure 4-3) and use the Search control at the top of the window.
- Use the Search box at the top-right corner of the Visual Basic Editor. (This is just to the right of the Menu.)

Just type the specific word or phrase with which you need help. When you press ENTER, the help system does its best to find something related to what you typed. It is a good idea to be as specific in your search term as you can. If you don't find any results with the first search, you can always alter the search so that it is more general in nature.

Navigating the Help System

Take a look at a typical help system window, as shown in Figure 4-3. Notice that there are a group of buttons across the top of the window that allow you to navigate through the help file, reading information as you would in a book. In fact, the most helpful tool is the one that looks like a book. Click it and you'll see an outline at the left side of the help window. You can then use the outline to help explore the information available.

The Visual Basic Editor provided with Word 2007 and Word 2010) uses the standard Windows help system to display information. In Word 2013 you'll find that the help system is online-based, giving you access to the MSDN Library. (MSDN is an pseudo-acronym for *Microsoft Developer Network.*) To fully describe all the features of the Windows help system would require an entire chapter in this book. It is a powerful tool that many VBA programmers come to depend on heavily while writing their programs. If you have never used the Windows help facility, you should take some time to explore it. When you need assistance, on-line help is usually the fastest way to get it.

Customizing How VBA Works

Given the same office, no two individuals will organize it the same way. John may like his desk by the window and Jane may prefer hers facing the door. The Visual Basic Editor is so advanced that it allows you to customize virtually any aspect of the environment. Some of the changes you make may apply only to your current project, while other changes apply to all your projects.

Program Options

The Visual Basic Editor provides a great deal of flexibility that you can harness to control how the program works. For instance, some people may find that the default font used in the Code window is a bit too small for their taste. This—and many other program elements—can easily be changed as you desire.

To access these options, choose Options from the Tools menu. The Options dialog box is displayed, as shown in Figure 4-4.

Note that the Options dialog box includes four different tabs. Each of these contains a variety of options that you can modify, as you desire.

- **Editor.** This tab allows you to modify how the editor responds to what you type in the Code window. For the most part, you won't want to change anything here. The one possible exception is to enable the

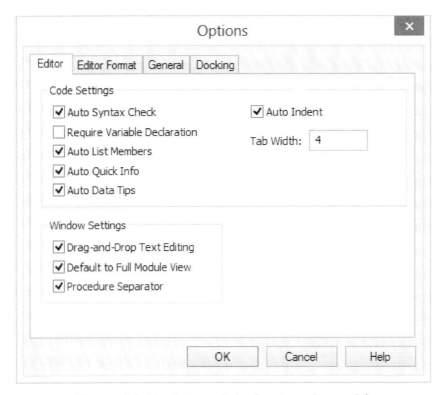

Figure 4-4. The Options dialog box is used to modify how you work with the Visual Basic Editor.

Require Variable Declaration check box. Doing so forces you to declare variables in your programs, which is always good programming practice.

- **Editor Format.** This tab includes options that control the format of what you see in the Code window. Font size and color for various types of text are the primary options you can affect.
- **General.** Using the controls on this tab specifies when the editor compiles the code you enter and what it should do if it detects errors.
- **Docking.** The various elements of the Visual Basic Editor, described earlier in this chapter, can be "docked" so that they cling to one of the sides of the program window. Docking is generally a good thing, but if you don't want some element to be dockable, you can control it on this tab.

The best thing to do is to remember that you can modify how the Visual Basic Editor does its work. As you become more familiar with the editor, you may want to modify various aspects of the environment to fit your desires. The first place to check for what can be changed is the Options dialog box.

Project Properties

Project properties are those options which affect the VBA project on which you are currently working. To change the options for the current project, choose the Project Properties option from the Tools menu. (The name of the menu option depends on what you have selected in the Project Explorer. The option will always end with "Properties," however.) The Project Properties dialog box appears, as shown in Figure 4-5.

There are two tabs in the Project Properties dialog box—General and Protection. The first tab allows you to change the project name and provide a description for the project. It also allows you to associate a help file with the project and specify parameters that affect how your code is compiled by the editor. Most macro programmers don't really mess with anything on this tab; it is usually used by those who are writing full-blown VBA programs that are destined to operate as Word add-ons.

The second tab, Protection, allows you to change parameters that affect who can see and change your programming code. For macros destined to be used

Word VBA Guidebook

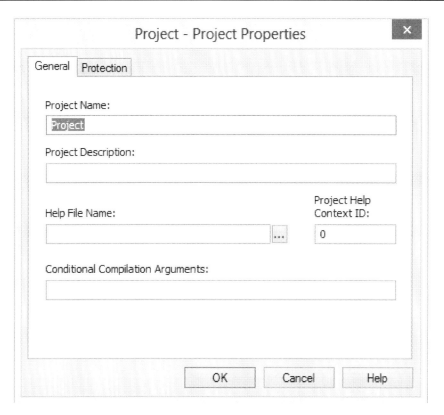

Figure 4-5. *The Project Properties dialog box allows you to modify elemental aspects of your VBA project.*

solely on your computer system, this probably isn't necessary. It may be necessary, however, if you are creating macros that you place in a template for use by others in your organization.

Quitting the Visual Basic Editor

When you are done working in the Visual Basic Editor, you'll probably want to close it so that you can either quit Word or start to work on a different document. There are three ways you can close the editor:

- Click the red Close button at the upper-right corner of the program window.
- Choose Close and Return to Microsoft Word from the File menu.
- Press ALT+Q.

Any of these methods of quitting the Visual Basic Editor will do just fine. You may, however, want to make sure that you save your changes before leaving the editor. Most of the time this may not seem like a big deal. After all, your macro modules are stored in either templates or documents, so they are saved automatically when you later, in Word, save the template or document at point. However, I've known many people who wish they had explicitly saved their changes, in the Visual Basic Editor, when something unexpected happened in Word that made saving impossible.

The typical way of saving your changes is to click the disk tool on the Visual Basic Editor Toolbar. This results in the saving of whatever project (document or template) is currently selected in the Project Explorer.

Managing Macros

When you start creating macros, it isn't long before you realize that you can use macros for a wide range of purposes. Before you know it, you'll have dozens of macros that do everything from small tasks to major document processing. This presents a problem, however—what do you do with all those macros?

The answer is that you manage them and integrate them into your use of Word so that they are easier than ever to use. This chapter covers some of the topics that can make you even more productive with your macros:

- How to add macros to your toolbars
- How to create and change shortcut keys associated with macros
- Using the Organizer to manage your macro modules
- Exporting and importing macro code

Adding Macros to Word's Interface

Earlier, in Chapter 3, you learned that you can edit Word's built-in commands and that doing so could change how Word accomplishes its regular tasks. This implies that Word's tools (visible on the Quick Access Toolbar and on various ribbon tabs) are made up of macro commands. This implication is close to the truth, although it is more technically correct to say that the capabilities of Word's functions are accessible through macro code.

What does this have to do with your macros? Quite a bit, really. If you can access Word's commands through toolbars and through your macros, is there a way to add the macros you create to Word's interface? The answer is a resounding yes, depending on the version of Word you are using. The following sections examine how you can make the changes for your macros.

Adding Macros to the Quick Access Toolbar

Word is a very flexible program and a big part of that flexibility is due to macros. If you create a macro, you may want to add it to the Quick Access Toolbar so that you can quickly run it whenever you want. To add it, follow these steps:

1. Display the Word Options dialog box. (In Word 2007 click the Office button and then click Word Options. In Word 2010 and Word 2013 display the File tab of the ribbon and then click Options.)
2. At the left side of the dialog box, click Customize (Word 2007) or Quick Access Toolbar (Word 2010 and Word 2013).
3. Using the Choose Commands From drop-down list, choose Macros (see Figure 5-1).
4. In the list of available macros, select the one you want assigned to the Quick Access Toolbar.
5. Click the Add button. The command now appears at the right side of the dialog box.
6. Click the OK button. The command now appears on the Quick Access Toolbar.

Take another look at what you see in Figure 5-1. The macros shown in the left side of the dialog box may look a bit strange to you. The names aren't the short names that you gave the macros when you created them. Instead, they are a much longer name that consists of project and module names. In the case of those shown in Figure 5-1, "Normal" is the project name and NewMacros is the module name. You can also see both the project name and module name in the Visual Basic Editor's Project Explorer. In the Word Options dialog box each "level" of hierarcy for the macros are separated by periods. The very right-most

Chapter 5: Managing Macros

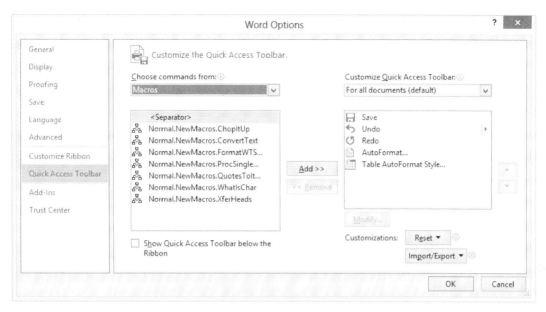

Figure 5-1. *The Word Options dialog box allows you to customize what is shown on the Quick Access Toolbar.*

portion of each macro is the actual macro name that you specified for your macro when you created it.

By default Word stores your customization so that it is available to all documents that you may open in Word. If you want the customization to be available to only a single document or to a template, you can use the Customize Quick Access Toolbar drop-down list to specify your wishes. The drop-down list is located just above the right column of the dialog box.

In addition, you'll probably want to modify the icon that Word uses on the Quick Access Toolbar for your macro. This is easy to do; all you need to do is click on the macro in the right column of the dialog box and then click the Modify button. (The Modify button is grayed out in Figure 5-1. It is only available if a macro is selected in the right side of the dialog box.) Word displays the Modify Button dialog box, shown in Figure 5-2.

Using the dialog box you can select from one of the many icons available for macros. When you click OK, Word makes the assignment.

Figure 5-2. You can change the icon that Word uses for your macro.

Adding Macros to Ribbon Tabs

If you are using Word 2010 or Word 2013 you can also add your macro to various tabs on the ribbon. This capability is not available in Word 2007. (Actually, you can change the ribbon tools in Word 2007, but the steps to do it involve quite a bit of XML gyrations and are beyond the scope of this book.)

1. Display the File tab of the ribbon.
2. Click Options. Word displays the Word Options dialog box.
3. At the left side of the dialog box click Customize Ribbon.
4. Using the Choose Commands From drop-down list, choose Macros (see Figure 5-3).
5. At the right side of the dialog box, use the plus and minus icons to display the place on the ribbons where you want your macro to appear. Each item that possesses a plus or minus icon is considered a group.

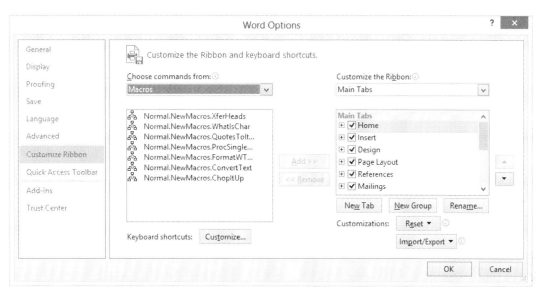

Figure 5-3. Word 2010 and Word 2013 users can add their macros to any of the tabs on the ribbon.

6. Select the group after which you want your macro to appear.

7. Click the New Group button. Word adds a group to the ribbon, right after the group you selected in step 6. This group is used to contain your macros. Note that the new group should now be selected.

8. Click the Rename button. Word displays the Rename dialog box, which looks very similar to the Modify Button dialog box shown in Figure 5-2.

9. Modify the name of the group, as desired, in the Display Name box.

10. Click OK to close the Rename dialog box. Your new group should still be selected in the Word Options dialog box.

11. In the list of available macros (left side of the dialog box) select the one you want added to your new group.

12. Click the Add button. The command now appears at the right side of the dialog box.

13. Click the OK button. The command now appears on the ribbon at the point where you added it.

Note that you can change the icon used for the command by using the Modify button after step 12, the same as described in the previous section.

Creating Shortcut Keys for Macros

Word allows you to easily assign macros to specific key combinations. These key combinations are referred to as *shortcut keys*, and they allow you to run the macro simply by using the shortcut key. When you first create a macro by recording it, Word gives you the opportunity to assign the macro to a specific key combination. You do this by using the Keyboard button in the Record Macro dialog box.

In my experience, most people don't assign a shortcut key to a macro right off the bat. Instead, they wait to make sure the macro is going to work and then they assign a shortcut key to the existing macro. Follow these steps:

1. Display the Word Options dialog box. (In Word 2007 click the Office button and then click Word Options. In Word 2010 and Word 2013 display the File tab of the ribbon and then click Options.)
2. At the left side of the dialog box, click Customize (Word 2007) or Customize Ribbon (Word 2010 and Word 2013).
3. Near the bottom of the dialog box click the Customize button. Word displays the Customize Keyboard dialog box.
4. Scroll through the Categories list and select the Macros category. The list at the right side of the dialog box changes to show the currently available macros, as shown in Figure 5-4.
5. In the Macros list, select the macro you want assigned to the shortcut key.
6. With the insertion point in the Press New Shortcut Key box, press the shortcut key you want to use. For instance, if you want to use CTRL+ALT+J, press that.
7. Just below the Current Keys box you can see whether the shortcut key is already assigned to a different function.
8. Click on Assign.

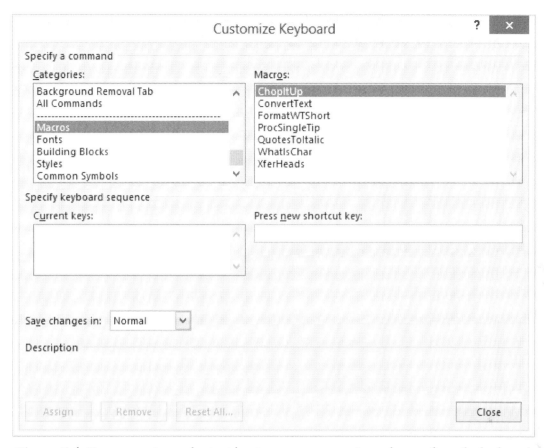

Figure 5-4. *You can assign a shortcut key to your macro so it can be run from the keyboard.*

9. Repeat steps 5 through 8 for each change you want to make.
10. Click on Close.

If you later want to remove the association between the shortcut key and the macro, you can follow the same steps. The only exception is that in step 5 you'll notice in the Current Keys box the list of current shortcut key assignments for the macro. You just have to select the key assignment you want to remove and then click the Remove button.

It is worth mentioning that how macros are displayed in the Customize Keyboard dialog box (Figure 5-4) is different from the way they are displayed when customizing the Quick Access Toolbar (Figure 5-1) or the ribbons (Figure 5-3).

If you compare the dialog boxes you'll notice that the Customize Keyboard dialog box shows the short name of each macro—the name you gave each of them—without the project name and module name.

Using the Organizer

Word provides the ability to work with templates, which in turn allow you to associate styles and macros with a particular document. This is very powerful, and provides a great deal of flexibility to Word. Sometimes, however, it can be a real pain to get a good "overall" view of what you have available in a particular template or even in a document.

This is where the Organizer comes into play. Word provides the Organizer (a deceptively simple name) to allow you complete control over what styles and macros are in a template or a document. While you don't use the Organizer to create any of these items, you can use it to copy them from one template or document to another, or to delete them completely.

The Organizer is used to manage macros at a module level. In Chapter 2 you discover what modules are and that macros are stored within modules. The Organizer lets you work with those modules; follow these steps:

1. Press **ALT+F8**. Word displays the Macros dialog box.
2. At the bottom of the dialog box click the Organizer button. Word displays the Organizer.
3. Make sure the Macro Project Items tab is selected, as shown in Figure 5-5.
4. Examine the left and right side of the Organizer. Each side can display modules in either a document or a template.
5. Use the pull-down lists on either the left or right to indicate the template or document whose macros or modules you want to manage.
6. If you cannot locate the desired template or document using the pull-down lists, click on the Close button on one side to "free up" an area. Then click on the Open button to locate and open the desired template or document.

Chapter 5: Managing Macros

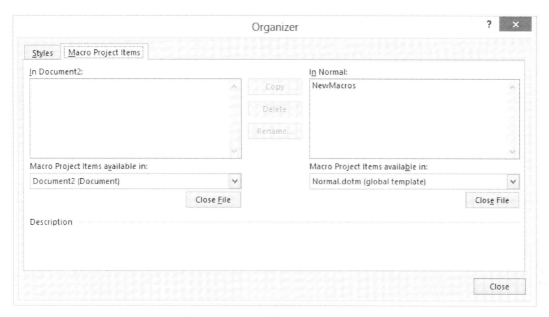

Figure 5-5. The Organizer allows you to manage the various macro modules in your documents and templates.

7. Select the module you want to copy, rename, or delete.

8. Click on the Copy button to copy the module to the other document or template. If the target file already has a module with the name of the one being copied, you are asked if you want to replace it.

9. Click on the Rename button to change the name of the selected module. The Organizer prompts you for a new name.

10. Click on the Remove button to delete the module. The Organizer asks you to confirm your action. (This is a very good thing, as there can be many, many macros in a module.)

11. Repeat steps 7 through 10 for each module you want to affect.

12. Click on Close when done.

Exporting Macros

You already know that macros are stored in documents or in templates and that you use the Visual Basic Editor to make changes to the macros. One often overlooked feature of the editor, however, is the ability to export macros to their own file. The Visual Basic Editor allows you to export to a plain-text file, one that can be opened with any text editor, such as Notepad.

You can't export individual macros, but you can export entire modules of macros. You do it by following these steps:

1. Press ALT+F11 to display the Visual Basic Editor.
2. Use the Project Explorer to select the module you want to export.
3. Choose Export File from the File menu. Word displays the Export File dialog box, shown in Figure 5-6.
4. Provide a filename for the export file. (Note that files should use the .Bas filename extension. This indicates that the file contains Visual Basic programming instructions.)

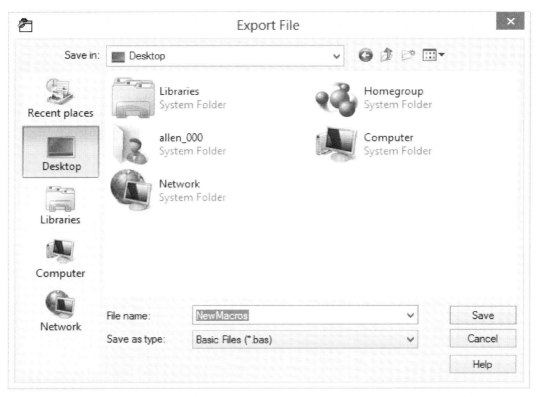

Figure 5-6. Exporting a module to a text file is easy using the editor's Export File feature.

5. Use the controls in the dialog box to select the folder in which you want the export file saved.
6. Click Save.

That's it; the module remains in the Visual Basic Editor, but now you also have a text file on your hard drive that contains the code. You can open the file with any text editor—just right-click on it and choose to open with Notepad.

It is a good idea to export macros if you want to easily move them from your system to an entirely different computer system. All you need to do is store the exported code in a place where you can access it from the other system, such as a network drive or a thumb drive. You can then follow the instructions in the next section to import the module to the other system.

If your module has quite a few macros in it and you only want a single macro out of the module, then exporting may be overkill. Instead you should consider simply copying the macro to a text file. You can do this by simply selecting the procedure in the Code window, pressing **Ctrl+C** to copy it to the Clipboard, and then pasting the procedure into a text file you create in Notepad.

Importing Macros

Importing macros is the opposite of exporting them. If you want to import a module, you can do it by just following a few simple steps:

1. Press **Alt+F11** to display the Visual Basic Editor.
2. Use the Project Explorer to select the project into which you want the module imported.
3. Choose Import File from the File menu. Word displays the Import File dialog box, which looks very much like a standard Open dialog box.
4. Use the controls in the dialog box to locate and select the module you want to import.
5. Click the Open dialog box.

The module is loaded from the file and attached to the project you specified in step 2.

You should note that you should only try to import modules you previously exported using the instructions in the previous section. If you try to import a module created in some other way, you may be at the mercy of how the Visual Basic Editor parses that file. If it contains errors, it can cause problems with the project that contains it.

Using VBA's Built-In Functions

VBA offers an extremely rich set of built-in functions for manipulating dates, times, strings, and numbers. Built-in functions are important because they save you time and effort—you don't need to reinvent the wheel.

In this chapter you discover how to use functions in your programs. You'll learn the syntax and nuances of various functions that can make your programming life easier. By the time you reach the end of this chapter, you'll know how functions are used.

Not all VBA functions are covered in this chapter. (There wouldn't be enough room!) Some of the functions that are not discussed in this chapter include financial calculations, advanced mathematical operations (such as transcendental functions), error-handling functions, and a bunch of miscellaneous functions. All the fundamental functions you need to develop most of your programs, however, are included.

The Benefits of Functions

It doesn't take much thought to recognize the benefits of using built-in functions. For example, imagine how long it would take to accomplish the seemingly simple task of determining whether today is Monday. You would have to figure out how to get the date from your PC, find a formula for calculating the day of the week given that date, and write a small program to implement it. But VBA's Weekday function returns the day of the week in one easy step.

To continue the example, if there weren't built-in functions for working with dates, you would have to buy or borrow reference material on PC internals in order to know where and how the date is stored. You would also need to figure out a way to access the specific memory location containing the date and time information—not an easy task since VBA has no inherent means of accessing a specific memory location. There are third-party tools to give you access to memory, but you would still need a formula to calculate the day of the week. Even if you already had these items, it would take at least an hour to write the program and test it. In contrast, it takes only a moment to find the built-in function you need and incorporate it in your program.

Date and Time Functions

How many days have passed since your birth? On what day of the week is Christmas next year? How long until your anniversary? When will your home mortgage be paid off? The answers to these questions require the ability to work with dates.

To determine how many days have passed since your birth, you must subtract your birth date from the current date. VBA has a function to calculate the difference between two dates, and you'll see an example of it later in this chapter. VBA also has functions that allow you to answer the other questions as well.

VBA's date functions work with dates ranging from before 1,900 years ago to about 7,000 years in the future.

Time is important to everyone on some scale. For a military operation, accuracy is often required to the second—or less; for a busy executive, every minute counts. Most people, however, are probably concerned with at least the hour. Even while on vacation you must stay conscious of the date and time, or you may be late returning to your more hectic life.

It's no wonder then that PCs keep track of both the date and time. VBA provides a variety of functions that allow you to access and manipulate both the date and time. Each function typically returns or uses the date and time stored in a variable using the Variant data type (see Chapter 2). This provides you with information you can readily use in your programs.

How VBA Stores Times and Dates

If you started a stopwatch at this moment and stopped it in 315,360,000 seconds how much older would you be? Because humans don't have the lightning-fast calculating speed of computers, it isn't very easy for us to make such calculations. With the aid of a calculator, you'll quickly see that you would be about 10 years older (not accounting for leap years).

What significant historical event occurred approximately 735,000 days ago? Again, most of us are at a loss. A properly programmed computer, however, would quickly determine the year as 0 AD. With that information you know that either the birth or death of Christ was the event (depending on which religious scholars you question).

VBA handles date ranges of this magnitude quite handily by storing dates and times as a serial number in a double-precision number. Everything to the left of the decimal point represents the date and everything to the right represents the time.

You may remember from Chapter 2 that the range of numbers that can be stored in this data type is quite large; VBA can handle dates that cover approximately a 10,000 year range. The portion of the date value to the left of the decimal point represents the number of days since January 1, 100. If you converted the date value to a double-precision floating-point number (a Double data type), the value for January 1, 100, is represented as -657,434; the value for January 2, 100, is -657,433; the value for January 3, 100, is -657,432; and so on up through December 31, 9999, which is 2,958,465. That is a span of 2,615,899 values (days), or just slightly under 9,899 years.

The following macro illustrates the range of dates that can be used in VBA:

```
Sub ShowDates()
    Dim dblMyNum As Double
    Dim J As Integer
    Dim sTemp As String
```

```
    ' Put together early dates
    sTemp = ""
    For J = 0 To 4
        dblMyNum = -657434 + J
        sTemp = sTemp & Format(dblMyNum, "mm/dd/yyyy")
        sTemp = sTemp & "  =  " & dblMyNum & vbCrLf
    Next J

    ' Put together future dates
    sTemp = sTemp & vbCrLf
    For J = 0 To 4
        dblMyNum = 2958461 + J
        sTemp = sTemp & Format(dblMyNum, "mm/dd/yyyy")
        sTemp = sTemp & "  =  " & dblMyNum & vbCrLf
    Next J

    MsgBox sTemp
End Sub
```

This macro uses several a For loop to do its work; this looping structure is discussed more fully in Chapter 7. In addition it also uses the Format function, which is described at the end of this chapter. The result of running the macro is shown in Figure 6-1.

Determining Today's Date

The Date function is the starting point for many calculations involving dates. For instance, if you want to know how long ago a certain date was or how far in the future a certain date will be, you must start with today's date.

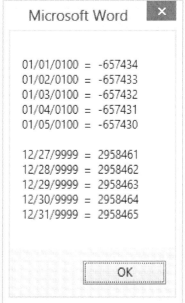

Figure 6-1. *Illustrating the range of dates supported in VBA.*

The format of the Date function is as follows:

```
Date
```

Pretty simple, huh? The value returned by the function is a Variant that can be stored in a variable in this manner:

```
Dim dTodaysDate As Date
dTodaysDate = Date
```

After this code is executed you can use dTodaysDate for any other calculations you desire or for displaying information to the screen.

Remember that when you use the Date function, the date returned is the date stored in the PC's internal clock. If the date stored in the PC is wrong, then the Date function obviously doesn't return the correct date.

Determining the Current Time

If you must know the current time of day, use the Time function. This is helpful if you need to record the starting time of some process you are about to perform or if you want to grab the time so you can add it to your document's text. The use of the Time function is just as simple as the use of the Date function:

```
Dim dCurrentTime As Date
dCurrentTime = Time
```

Note that the value returned by the Time function is, again, a serial value. It is essentially a date serial number with the portion to the left of the decimal point set to 0. Because it is a date serial number you can store it in a variable that uses the Date data type.

Getting Both the Time and Date

Sometimes you need both today's date and the current time. You could use both the Date and Time functions, but there is a simpler way. You can use the Now function, which combines both Date and Time functions. Again, it is just as simple to use as both the Date and Time functions:

```
Dim dTimeDate As Date
dTimeAndDate = Now
```

Now is probably convenient for timing the execution of your program. To find out how long part of your program takes to execute, you could use code in the following manner:

```
Dim dStartTime As Date
Dim dTotalTime As Date
dStartTime = Now
```

```
'code to be timed here

dTotalTime = Now - dStartTime
```

Make sure that the section you are timing doesn't contain anything that depends on user input (such as a button press or text entry) because it distorts the timing (unless of course, you want to time how long it takes for the user to respond).

Extracting Part of the Date

Sometimes you only need part of the date. For questions such as "Is today Wednesday?" and "Is this 2011?" VBA provides the following four functions for extracting only the part of the date in which you're interested:

- The Year function returns the year portion of the date. (The range could be 100 to 9999.)
- The Month function returns an integer from 1 to 12 (January to December).
- The Day function returns the day of the month (1 to 31).
- The Weekday function returns the day of the week represented by a number from 1 to 7 (Sunday to Saturday).

The format used by these functions is as follows:

```
Dim iThisYear As Integer
Dim iThisMonth As Integer
Dim iThisDay As Integer
Dim iDoW As Integer

iThisYear = Year(Date)
iThisMonth = Month(Now)
iThisDay = Day(Date)
iDoW = Weekday(Now)
```

After these code lines are executed iThisYear contains an integer value of the current year, such as 2013; iThisMonth contains an integer value of the current month, such as 12; iThisDay contains an integer value of the current day, such as 30; and iDoW is in the range 1 to 7, where 1 represents Sunday, 2 represents Monday, and so on through 7, which represents Saturday.

Displaying a Weekday Name

If someone asks you "When was the last time you used your PC?" would you answer "Last 3."? No, of course not. For calculation purposes, the integers returned by the Weekday function work just fine, but for display they just won't do. That's where the WeekdayName function comes into play.

```
Sub TypeWeekday()
    Dim iDoW As Integer

    iDoW = Weekday(Now)
    Selection.TypeText WeekdayName(iDoW)
End Sub
```

Remember that the Weekday function returns a number of 1 through 7, which corresponds to Sunday through Saturday. The WeekdayName function takes that number and returns a full weekday name, such as Monday, Tuesday, etc. If you run this example, the macro types today's weekday name into the current document.

Extracting Part of the Time

If you were only interested in a portion of the time (for example, the hour), you could use VBA's string functions to separate out the part in which you were interested.

Given the time 7:45:05 you could use InStr (a text function discussed later in this chapter) to find the first and second colon. Then, depending on which portion of the time you were interested in, you could use the Mid function (again, described later in this chapter) to obtain that part. An easier way, however, is by using any of the following functions: Hour, Minute and Second.

```
Dim iThisHour As Integer
Dim iThisMinute As Integer
Dim iThisSecond As Integer

iThisHour = Hour(Now)
iThisMinute = Minute(Now)
iThisSecond = Second(Now)
```

When this example is executed, iThisHour contains an integer value of the current hour, from 0 and 23; iThisMinute contains an integer value of the current minute, between 0 and 59; and iThisSecond contains an integer value of the current second, also between 0 and 59.

Differences between Two Dates

Earlier in this chapter you learned that you could use one of VBA's built-in functions to determine the number of days since you were born. DateDiff is that function. The DateDiff function returns the number of days between two dates. If the first date is actually after the second, then DateDiff returns a negative number.

The format to use with this function is as follows:

```
DateDiff(interval, startdate, enddate)
```

Where *interval* is a string representing the units in which you want to measure the difference, *startdate* is the first date, and *enddate* is the second date. The *interval* value is specified as one of the following:

- yyyy (year)
- q (quarter)
- m (month)
- ww (week)
- y (day of year)
- w (weekday)
- d (day)
- h (hour)
- n (minute)
- s (second)

Remember that the *interval* must be expressed as a string, so here is one example of how you could use the function:

```
Dim NumDays As Variant

NumDays = DateDiff("d", Now, "6/5/86")
```

This example calculates the number of days since June 5, 1986.

Deriving a Date

To go the other way when you have a date and want to find a date in the future, it is best to use the DateAdd function. Its format is similar to the DateDiff function:

```
DateAdd(interval, number, date)
```

The *interval* is any of the same intervals that are used with the DateDiff function. The *number* parameter is how many of those units you want to add to the *date* parameter. Here's an example:

```
Dim dFutureDate As Date
Dim dPastDate As Date

dFutureDate = DateAdd("yyyy", 10, Now)
dPastDate = DateAdd("yyyy", -10, Now)
```

The first example sets dFutureDate to a date ten years in the future and the second example sets dPastDate to a date ten years in the past.

String Functions

You're going to start off the discussion of string functions with a short trip into the workings of your computer. Computers store all their information (even strings) as binary numbers. Binary means one of two states—either on or off, 1 or 0. Computers work in binary because the electronic switches of which they're made are only capable of storing a 1 or a 0 at any particular location.

The binary numbering system is also referred to as the *base two numbering system*. The value following the word *base* is the number of different values any one digit may have in that numbering system. In the decimal system (base 10), each digit can have a value from 0 to 9—that's ten possible values. In base two there are only two possible values—0 or 1.

To count in decimal, you start with a single digit. That digit contains the value 0. As you increment your count you increase the value in that first digit. When you reach the maximum value for that digit you reset it to 0 and increment the digit to the left. This process continues as long as necessary. Counting in base two follows the same rules, except there are fewer values to use in the digits. The first few binary numbers, corresponding to the decimal values 0 through 7, are as follows:

- 000
- 001
- 010
- 011
- 100
- 101
- 110
- 111

You can see how numbers could be stored using this system. But how does this relate to strings?

Characters are stored using a numeric code. By representing a character with a number, that number can be stored and later retrieved by the computer. When displayed, it is converted back into the character so that you can understand it. For instance, the numeric code for the capital letter *A* is 65 or, in base two, 1000001; for the lowercase letter *a* it is 97, or 1100001.

In order for computers made by different manufacturers to communicate with one another, a standard code was necessary for the representation of information. The first commonly used code for the interchange of computer information was ASCII (American Standard Code for Information Interchange). ASCII has codes only for the values 0 through 127. Windows (and thus VBA) understand ASCII, but they also understand more comprehensive coding systems that allow for the representation of many more characters.

Comparing Strings

VBA provides the StrComp function which allows you to quickly determine if two strings are equal. What about the following strings, however:

```
This is a test string
THIS IS A TEST STRING
```

If you use the normal comparison operators (Chapter 2) to do a comparison, these strings are not considered equal. With StrComp, however, you can instruct it to ignore the case of the letters in the string—it all depends on your needs. (If StrComp takes the case of the letters into account, it is considered *case-sensitive*.)

Here's how you use the StrComp function:

```
StrComp(string1, string2, [comparison type])
```

In this format *string1* and *string2* are the strings to compare and a *comparison type* of 0 performs a case-sensitive compare while a *comparison type* of 1 performs the comparison without regard to case. If the *comparison type* is omitted (remember that it is optional—that's what the [brackets] in the format example mean) then the normal default of 0 is used. The return values are:

- -1 if string1 < string2
- 0 if string1 = string2
- 1 if string1 > string2

Here's an example:

```
Dim iResult As Integer

iResult = StrComp("Test this", "TEST THIS", 1)
```

iResults contains a 0 because it was instructed to perform a case-insensitive comparison, so StrComp considers the strings equal to each other.

Converting Strings

More often than not, you'll need to make certain conversions in text strings used in your programs. For example, you may need to ensure that a last name contains an initial uppercase character or that a variable is stored in all uppercase so an exact match can be made. VBA's text conversion functions provide the means for easily manipulating strings.

Converting the Case of a String

For switching entire strings to all upper- or lowercase, the functions LCase and UCase work well. Pass the string to be converted to one of these functions, and a string is returned which is guaranteed to be all uppercase or lowercase (depending on which function is used).

To convert just a single character, separate that character, convert it, and then splice it back in. Listing 5.5 shows an example of capitalizing the initial letter of a word using UCase.

```
Dim sLower As String
Dim sProper As String

sLower = "herberger"
sProper = UCase(Left(sLower,1)) & Mid(sLower,2)
```

When this code is executed, the sProper variable contains the proper capitalization for the name: Herberger.

Converting Characters to Values

You can use the Asc function to convert a single character to its underlying numeric code. Asc returns an integer value which is the numeric value of first character in a string. Here's an example:

```
Dim iNumValue As Integer

iNumValue = Asc("C")
```

When this code is executed, iNumValue contains the value 67. If the string passed to the Asc function is longer than a single character then the function only pays attention to the first character of the string.

Converting Values to Characters

The Chr function does just the opposite of Asc—it converts a number into an actual character. It is just as easy to use as the Asc function, as well:

```
Dim sMyString As String

sMyString = Chr(67)
```

When this code is executed, sMyString contains the uppercase letter *C*.

Converting a String to a Number

There are times when you want to convert a string to a number. This comes in handy when you get input from a user in the form of a string, but you must convert it to a number to process it further.

The Val function converts the numbers in a string into a value. If the string contains any non-numeric characters, then only that portion of the string before the first non-numeric character is converted. Val also properly converts a negative sign or exponentiation sign.

Here's an example to show how it works:

```
Dim lNum As Long

lNum = Val("12345abcde")
```

When this code is executed, lNum contains the value 12345. Remember: The Val function stops its conversion at the first non-numeric character in the string.

Converting a Number to a String

Many times you'll want to convert a number to a string, which is the opposite of what you did with the Val function in the previous section. The Str function allows you to convert a number into a string, adding a sign placeholder at the beginning (a space if the number is positive or a minus sign if the number is negative). For example:

```
Dim iOrigNum As Integer
Dim sNumOut As String

iOrigNum = 9876
sNumOut = Str(iOrigNum)
```

When this code is executed, sNumOut contains the characters " 9876". Notice the leading space, which is a placeholder for a negative sign.

Creating Strings

Occasionally you'll need a string of characters that are all the same. For example, you may be printing a report and need a line of dashes across the page. There are many ways to generate a string of some number of a specific character, but two built-in VBA functions, Space and String, are the easiest.

For instance, suppose you need a string of dashes to add to your document and you want this string to be 40 characters wide. The following code inserts the dashes in your document, as desired:

```
Sub InsertDashes()
    Dim sDashes As String

    sDashes = String(40,"-")
    Selection.TypeText sDashes
End Sub
```

While you can pass a string containing more than one character, the String function uses only the first character of the string. For example, String(5, "ABC") returns "AAAAA" not "ABCABCABCABCABC".

Often the character you need is the space, so there is a special function just for generating strings comprised of only spaces—the Space function. The string you construct using Space is no different than the string you get using String with a space character. If you prefer, you can always use the String function and forget about Space. Here's an example of how to use it:

```
Dim sMySpaces As String

sMySpaces = Space(10)
```

This example returns a string consisting of 10 space characters.

Other String Functions

So far you have learned that VBA provides quite a few string functions. You have not learned them all, however. VBA also provides other functions that allow you to do things like determine the length of a string, determine if one string is contained within another, and extract different parts of a string.

Finding the Length of a String

It is often critical to know the length of a string. For example, if you are processing a document and you are stepping through each paragraph of that document, you'll need to know the length of each paragraph to determine if some processing can take place. The way you figure out the length of a string is with the Len function. Here's a way it can be used:

```
Dim sTemp As String
Dim J As Integer

For J = 1 To 5
    sTemp = ActiveDocument.Paragraphs(J).Range.Text
    If Len(sTemp) > 0 Then
        ' Do some sort of processing here
    End If
Next J
```

This example steps through the first five paragraphs of the document, examining the length of the text in each of the paragraphs. (A For loop, described in Chapter 7, is used to step through the paragraphs.) The part you want to focus on is the Len function, which checks the length of the sTemp string. If it is greater than 0 then the processing can occur.

Strings within Strings

Another thing you may often need to do is to check to see if one string is contained within another string. For instance, you might want to know if a particular string contains the word "at". One way you can do this is using the InStr function, which returns a number indicating where in the string another string occurs. If it does not occur, then the function returns a 0.

Here is an example of using the InStr function:

```
Sub CheckString()
    Dim sMyString As String
    Dim iLocation As Integer
    Dim sResult As String

    sMyString = "Where is the cat found at?"
    iLocation = InStr(sMyString, " at")
    sResult = "Didn't find it"
    If iLocation > 0 Then
        sResult = "Found it at character " & iLocation
```

```
        End If
        MsgBox sResult
End Sub
```

Note that what is searched for in this use of the InStr function is the string " at", with a leading space. This is to make sure that it finds a word beginning with the letters *at*; it precludes finding a match in the word *cat*.

Extracting the Ends and Middle of a String

If you only require the leftmost or rightmost portions of a word, then the Left and Right functions are the most convenient. All you need to do is tell VBA how many characters to strip from the string. If you want to pull characters from the middle of a string then you use the Mid function, which also requires a beginning location.

```
Dim sMyString As String
Dim sLeftPart As String
Dim sRightPart As String
Dim sMiddlePart As String

sMyString = "This is my very long string"
sLeftPart = Left(sMyString, 9)
sRightPart = Right(sMyString, 11)
sMiddlePart = Mid(sMyString, 9, 7)
```

Run this code and you find out that sLeftPart contains "This is m", sRightPart contains "long string", and sMiddlePart contains "my very".

You should note that both the Left and Right function only need to know how many characters to pull from the original string, but the Mid function needs both a starting character location (starting with character 1 of the string) and the number of characters to pull. If you don't provide a number of characters with the Mid function, then it returns the rest of the original string.

Math Functions

Mathematics is an important part of everyday life. You do simple math hundreds of times each day. You buy things and count your change, you calculate the mileage your new car is getting, and many more things involving simple math.

Sometimes the math you must do is a little more complex. If you're buying a house, you'll need more advanced functions to determine your payments, given a particular interest rate, amount borrowed, and loan duration. If you are a scientist, engineer, or machinist, or you have one of many occupations which require the use of more advanced functions, you'll appreciate the power inherent in VBA's math functions.

If you think math is too difficult or you don't have a practical use for it, consider some of the examples you are about to see. Everyone uses math to make life easier, and VBA provides you with the functions to perform that math more quickly and accurately.

Extracting an Integer

If you are just interested in the portion of a number to the left of the decimal point, Int returns it for you. This is handy in some mathematical calculations where you need to make sure you are working with whole numbers. Here's a simple example:

```
Dim dblMyLong As Double
Dim iMyInteger As Integer

dblMyLong = 52.94387
iMyInteger = Int(dblMyLong)
```

When this code is executed, iMyInteger contains the value 52. What if you're interested in only the decimal portion? Simple. Just subtract the Int part from the original number. The decimal portion remains:

```
Dim dblMyLong As Double
Dim iMyInteger As Integer
Dim dblMyDecimal As Double

dblMyLong = 52.94387
iMyInteger = Int(dblMyLong)
dblMyDecimal = dblMyLong - iMyInteger
```

Generating Random Numbers

Have you ever played a computer game where the computer deals cards, throws dice, or spins a roulette wheel? Did you ever wonder how the random outcome of those events was simulated? Using VBA's Rnd function you can easily generate random events.

Before using the Rnd function, you must understand that the random numbers generated by VBA are not truly random. This is why you may hear them referred to as *pseudo-random numbers*. A complete discussion of random numbers and the theory behind generating them would require a book at least as large as this one.

So, if you build a game of chance based on the random number generator in VBA and then develop a system which consistently beats your game, don't take your life savings to Las Vegas or Atlantic City—their games generate far more random numbers.

Here's a simple use of the Rnd function:

```
Dim sngHelterSkelter As Single

sngHelterSkelter = Rnd
```

The number returned by Rnd is equal to or greater than 0 and less than 1. You can also include an optional parameter with Rnd which affects the results returned. If the optional value is less than 0 then Rnd returns the same random number every time it is invoked. If the optional value is 0 then Rnd returns the same number as the last time it was used. Finally, if the optional value is greater than 0 then Rnd returns the next random number in its sequence. If you want to use one of these optional values (most people don't), then simply put it in parentheses after the function:

```
sngHelterSkelter = Rnd(0)
```

Something to be aware of when using VBA's random number generator is that each time the program is run, under ordinary circumstances the same series of numbers are generated. To ensure a different set of numbers, use the Randomize statement.

Typically, Randomize would be issued when your program is started, although it doesn't hurt to issue it as many times as you like. Randomize reseeds the random number generator resulting in a different sequence of numbers each time your program is run.

```
Dim sngHelterSkelter As Single

Randomize
sngHelterSkelter = Rnd
```

To generate random integers within a specific range, use the following formula:

```
Int((biggest - smallest + 1) * Rnd + smallest)
```

Where *biggest* is the largest integer you want returned and *smallest* is the lowest integer you want. Thus, if you wanted a random number between 50 and 75 you would use either of the following to assign the random value to the integer x:

```
x = Int((75 - 50 + 1) * Rnd + 50)
x = Int(26 * Rnd + 50)
```

Determining the Sign of a Number

When performing mathematical operations, it is sometimes necessary to know the sign of a number, or whether it is equal to zero. For example, before dividing a number by a variable, it is good to know whether that variable is equal to zero. If it is, then the result of the division is indeterminate and shouldn't be performed because an error would be generated in your program. If you are about to take an even root of a number, you most likely want to know if that number is negative.

The Sgn function determines whether a number is equal to, greater than, or less than zero all in one step. This is better than first testing the value to see if it is equal to zero and then testing to see if it was greater than zero or less than zero. The Sgn function is faster and more compact. One real purpose of the Sgn function is to determine whether a value is negative before textually formatting it.

```
Dim iMyValue As Integer
Dim sMyMessage As String
Dim iMySign As Integer

iMyValue = -3
iMySign = Sgn(iMyValue)
iMyMessage = "equal to zero"
If iMySign = 1 Then iMyMessage = "greater than one"
If iMySign = -1 Then iMyMessage = "less than one"
```

```
iMyMessage = Str(iMyValue) & " is " & iMyMessage
MsgBox iMyMessage
```

When this code is executed, iMySign contains -1 since the value being tested (iMyValue) is less than 0.

Positive Values

In some calculations, such as square roots, negative numbers are not acceptable (unless you are prepared to write special and highly complex routines for handling imaginary numbers—not an easy task in VBA). Sometimes the calculation can continue by ensuring the number is positive. You could test a number before using it and multiply it by -1 if it was negative, thereby changing its sign, but there is an easier way.

The guaranteed result of the Abs function is a positive number. This function returns the positive value of a number. Thus, if the number was originally negative, it is changed to positive. If the number was positive, it remains unchanged.

```
Sub FindSquareRoot()
    Dim dblResult As Double
    Dim sRawInput As String
    Dim dblSource As Double

    sRawInput = InputBox("What number?")
    dblSource = Val(sRawInput)
    If dblSource <> 0 Then
        dblResult = Sqr(Abs(dblSource))
        MsgBox "The result is " & dblResult
    End If
End Sub
```

Using the Abs function within the square root function guarantees that an error won't occur if UnknownVariable is negative.

Formatting

Formatting refers to the way in which you alter the looks of the information your program presents. The Format function allows you to easily format values for output. For example, consider the number 3.14159265359. When formatted as currency, it is shown as $3.14. When formatted as a percent, it is displayed as 314.16%. When formatted as a medium time, it gives 03:23 a.m. Formatting puts the number in context.

The format of the Format function is as follows:

```
Format(expression[, fmt])
```

In this format *expression* is a numeric or string expression and *fmt* is any of a wide range of different formats that can be applied. (For information on available formats, see the on-line help system.) Here's a quick example of how you can use it:

```
Dim dblDividends As Double
Dim sOutput As String

dblDividends = 4423.7463
sOutput = Format(dblDividends, "Currency")
```

In this example, the formatted string $4,423.75 is stored in the sOutput string. VBA doesn't limit you to predefined formats in this manner. You can also create your own formats, a task that is not terribly hard, but is beyond the scope of this book. You can find more information about custom formatting codes for the Format function in the VBA online help.

7

Controlling Program Flow

The real strength of the computer is not in its number crunching ability as much as its ability to make decisions.

VBA steps through your macro code one line at a time. In this sense, VBA follows the path you pave through your code. Decisions based on the comparison of two or more items allow your program to follow one path or another. The potential to pick execution paths is really what makes computers useful. Without this capability, a computer would just be an overgrown hand-held calculator.

VBA provides many ways for you to control how a program is executed. This chapter explores these flow-control statements and explains where each is appropriate.

Conditional Execution

In Chapter 2 you learn about comparison operators and how to use them in a program. One of the most common places where they are used is in conditional statements. These are programming statements that affect program execution based on the outcome of some sort of logical comparison. These types of statements are very fundamental to any programming language, and VBA is no exception.

There are four types of conditional statements in VBA. They are the If...Then statement, the Select Case structure, the Do-Loop clause, and the While-Wend clause. The following sections explain each of these statements.

If ... Then

If the phone rings, answer it. If the dog barks, call me. If I have enough, I'll buy lunch; otherwise, you can. We use a form of VBA's If...Then statement on a daily basis. In common use, we just leave out all the words for a completely formed If...Then clause, or we substitute other words with similar meaning.

Take a closer look at the sentences in the preceding paragraph. They are rewritten here in a more structured manner:

```
If the phone rings Then
    answer the phone.

If the dog barks Then
    call me.

If I have enough money Then
    I'll pay for lunch
Else
    you pay for lunch.
```

These examples look very much like the VBA syntax for the If...Then statement because making decisions in your macros is much like making the simple decisions you make every day. For this reason, If...Then statements usually feel very natural.

At its most simple form, the If...Then statement can be used on a single line, as shown in these two examples:

```
Dim iAge As Integer
Dim sPerson As String

If iAge < 13 Then sPerson = "Child"
If (iAge > 12) And (iAge < 21) Then sPerson = "Youth"
```

Note that the If clause uses some sort of comparison that evaluates to either True or False. You can include more than one comparison, as in the second example, but it still must all evaluate to True or False.

For most people, the multi-line version of If...Then is what is used in macros.

```
Dim iAge As Integer
Dim sPerson As String

If iAge > 20 Then
    sPerson = "Adult"
    Beep
End If
```

Between the start of the If...Then structure and the final End If statement, you can have as many lines of programming code as you want. You can get even more complex by using the ElseIf and Else statements within the structure. Here's an example where the Else statement is used:

```
Dim sSex As String
Dim sType As String

If sSex = "F" Then
    sType = "Female"
Else
    sType = "Male"
End If
```

In this example, the statements between If and Else are executed if the comparison is True. If the comparison is not True, then the statements between Else and End If are executed.

The ElseIf statement allows additional comparisons to occur within the If...Then structure. Here's an example:

```
Dim sSex As String
Dim sType As String

If sSex = "F" Then
    sType = "Female"
ElseIf sSex = "M" Then
    sType = "Male"
Else
    sType = "Unknown"
End If
```

When used with the ElseIf...Then clause, the instructions between If and ElseIf are executed when the conditions following the If statement are True. If they are False, however, the conditions after the ElseIf statement are evaluated. If the second condition evaluates True, the instructions between ElseIf and

EndIf (or the next ElseIf) are executed. If the structure contains an Else clause (as it does in this example) then the statements between Else and End If are executed only if the result of the last ElseIf were False.

Formatting If ... Then Structures

You should perform only the simplest of tasks with an If...Then statement on a single line. It is easier to pick out the statements being executed if you use the multi-line form. Besides, your code often grows in complexity as you add functionality to your programs, ultimately requiring the use of the multi-line form anyway.

In the examples provided in the previous section, notice the indentation of the instructions within the If...Then structure. This makes the code more readable. It also helps solve the problem of forgetting to put an End If at the end of the If clause. When the executed statements are indented, you can easily see if you have forgotten the End If.

Indentation is especially helpful with nested If clauses. You use a nested If clause when you must make multiple levels of decisions, as shown in this example:

```
If X < 25 Then
    If X\2 <> 0 Then
        If X\3 <> 0 Then
            MsgBox "X is prime."
        End If
    End If
End If
```

At first glance, this example doesn't seem to offer any advantage over the following example code:

```
If (X < 25) And (X\2 <> 0) And (X\3 <> 0) Then
    MsgBox "X is prime."
End If
```

There are advantages, however, in nesting the If...Then structures. For instance, consider the example shown here:

```
If X < 25 Then
    MsgBox "Likelihood X prime is 10/24"
    If X\2 <> 0 Then
        MsgBox "Likelihood X prime is now 10/13"
        If X\3 <> 0 Then
            MsgBox "X is prime."
        End If
    End If
End If
```

The nested If gives you the opportunity to do additional work between checking each condition.

Using Not With If...Then

The use of Not can sometimes make an If statement more readable. For example, consider the following simple code which checks to see of a variable contains a False value or not.

```
Dim bHome As Boolean

bHome = True

    ' statements

If bHome = False Then
    MsgBox "No one here!"
End If
```

You can make your code a bit more understandable and shorter if you use the Not operator in your If...Then structure:

```
Dim bHome As Boolean

bHome = True

    ' statements

If Not bHome Then
    MsgBox "No one here!"
End If
```

The code in both of these examples works the same because conditions in an If...Then structure always evaluate to True or False. The Not operator negates, or switches, the logical condition of an expression—thus, Not True equals False and Not False equals True. If you plan the names of your variables and what they contain, your code can be much easier to read. Code that is easy to read allows you to concentrate on solving the problem at hand; it also is easier for others to understand.

Select Case

Many of the problems encountered while programming require long and often complicated If...Then statements. For example, the following code is required to determine which digit (1 to 5) a single digit number is. This code would be twice as long if checking for ten digits. It would be almost five times as long if checking for every character of the alphabet.

```
Dim iDigit As Integer
Dim sTemp As Integer

If iDigit = 1 Then
    sTemp= "One"
ElseIf iDigit = 2 Then
    sTemp= "Two"
ElseIf iDigit = 3 Then
    sTemp= "Three"
ElseIf iDigit = 4 Then
    sTemp= "Four"
ElseIf iDigit = 5 Then
    sTemp= "Five"
End If
```

One of the most convenient program flow constructs is the Select Case structure, which you can use to get rid of all those If...Then conditions. It is easy to use and provides a good solution to a wide variety of problems. Here's an example of the structure in action:

```
Dim iAge As Integer
Dim sPerson As String

iAge = 7

Select Case iAge
    Case Is < 13
        sPerson = "Child"
    Case Is < 20
        sPerson = "Teenager"
```

```
    Case Is >= 20
        sPerson = "Adult"
End Select
```

Note that the start of the Select Case structure includes something (in this case the iAge variable) that is tested in each Case statement within the structure. The expression that follows any Case statement can be in one of four forms:

- A numeric or string expression such as Val(iMyNum) or sFront.
- An explicit value such as 3 or True.
- A range of values by using the To keyword as in "A" To "Z" or 5 To 9.
- A conditional range of values by using the Is keyword such as Is < 0 or Is <> 0.

If the expression used in one of the Case statements matches the value of whatever is being tested in the Select Case statement, then the statements associated with that Case clause, and only the statements associated with that Case clause, are executed.

When using the Select Case statement, it is good practice to account for all anticipated cases with specific Case clauses and use the Case Else clause to flag an error if an unexpected value is encountered. If you use the Else clause to handle expected values, VBA processes any unexpected values possibly leading to erroneous results or unanticipated errors.

Switch

The Select Case statement allows only one test expression, and all the Cases must be related to that single test expression. Switch is different in that you can test different test expressions within the same function. You do this by simply defining a series of expressions to evaluate and what should be returned if the expression is True. The Switch statement allows you to define up to seven comparisons and values for those comparisons. Here's an example that uses five pairs:

```
Dim sLabel As String
Dim sOpVal As String
```

```
sLabel = "Operation is " & Switch(sOpVal = "+", "Addition", _
                                  sOpVal = "-", "Subtraction", _
                                  sOpVal = "*", "Multiplication", _
                                  sOpVal = "/", "Division", _
                                  True, "an Error")
```

When done, sLabel is equal to a value dependent on what is in the sOpVal variable. VBA evaluates the test expressions from left to right. When VBA encounters the first True expression, it doesn't evaluate any further.

Did you notice that the last condition in the Switch function example is always True? To catch any possible errors in expected values, place a statement at the end of the switch that always evaluates True.

Looping Structures

Besides conditional statements, VBA also includes several different types of structures, or *constructs*, which allow you to repeatedly execute segments of code as long as certain conditions (which you specify) are met. These types of constructs can add real power to your macros.

For looping structures, VBA provides the following:

- For loops
- For Each loops
- Do loops
- While loops

By effectively using these four types of constructs, you can create tight, concise code that still accomplishes a great deal of work. The following sections describe each of these constructs.

For Loop

The For loop is probably the control structure you'll use the most in you macros. It is a compact way to execute a set of instructions a certain number of times. You can use Do loop and a counter variable, but a For loop is more convenient. This example shows the simple way in which the For loop is used:

```
Dim sFull As String
Dim J As Integer

sFull = ""
For J = 1 To 10
    sFull = sFull & " " & Chr(64 + J)
Next J
```

The For loop is executed ten times, and each time through the loop the value of J (which is the loop counter) is equal to one of the values, 1 through 10. When this code has executed, sFull is equal to " A B C D E F G H I J".

It is permissible to omit the counter variable after the Next keyword in a For loop. Try to resist the temptation to do this, however. Using the variable name helps to match the Next with its For when you have multiple or nested For loops.

Incrementing the Loop Counter

Within a For loop the statements are always executed before the loop counter is incremented. If the increment causes the loop counter value to exceed the ending value, then the loop is exited. Otherwise it is executed again.

While it is possible to modify the value of a loop counter in a For loop, it can make following the execution of code difficult. Try to structure your code so this isn't necessary.

The loop counter is incremented by 1 each time through the For loop, unless you specify a Step value. Specifying a negative Step value causes the loop counter to be decremented. Here's an example of counting backward through a For loop:

```
Dim sFull As String
Dim J As Integer

sFull = ""
For J = 10 To 5 Step -1
    sFull = sFull & Chr(64 + J)
Next J
```

When this code has completed execution, the sFull variable contains the string "JIHGFE".

The loop test is not actually for equality, which can lead to potential problems. The following code results in the message dialog box displaying the values 1, 4, 7, and 10. The values contained in J through the loop are 1, 4, 7, 10, and finally 13. The For loop compares 13 to the ending value of 12 and because 13 is larger than 12, the loop terminates. If a For loop actually required an exact match on the final pass, it could enter an endless loop where the condition necessary for its termination was never met.

```
Dim J As Integer

For J = 1 To 12 Step 3
    MsgBox J
Next J
```

With a positive Step value the loop terminates when the counter is greater than the end value. If the Step value is negative, then the loop terminates when the counter is less than the end count.

Nesting a For Loop

For loops can be nested. This has certain advantages over a single For loop. A great example is if you are accessing each cell in a table stored in your Word document. The rows could easily be considered the outer loop and then each cell in that row would be handled by an inner loop. Here's an example:

```
Dim J As Integer
Dim K As Integer
Dim iNumRows As Integer
Dim iNumCols As Integer
Dim sChkTxt As String

'Loop to select each row in the current table
For J = 1 To iNumRows
    'Loop to select each cell in the current row
    For K = 1 To iNumCols
        'Select the cell to check
        Selection.Tables(1).Rows(J).Cells(K).Select
        'Copy any text in the cell
        sChkTxt = Selection.Text
        'Strip off the last 2 characters (removes end of cell marker)
        sChkTxt = Left(sChkTxt, Len(sChkTxt) - 2)
        'If empty, add "N/A" text
        If (sChkTxt = "") Then Selection.TypeText ("N/A")
    Next K
Next J
```

The total number of times the statements in the inner loop of a nested For loop execute is equal to the product of all the individual For loop iterations. In this case the total number of iterations is equal to iNumRows multiplied by iNumCols.

For Each Loop

One special type of control structure is available because of the object-oriented nature of VBA. You learn in Chapter 2 that Word makes objects and collections of objects available to your macro. The For Each loop provides an easy way to be able to step through each object within a collection of objects.

As an example, let's say you wanted to look through each paragraph in your document. You might want to find paragraphs in which there is a border set. The following macro does that:

```
Sub SearchForBorders()
    Dim K As Word.Paragraph
    Dim bFound As Boolean

    For Each K In ActiveDocument.Paragraphs
        bFound = False
        If K.Borders(wdBorderTop).LineStyle <> wdLineStyleNone _
          Then bFound = True
        If K.Borders(wdBorderLeft).LineStyle <> wdLineStyleNone _
          Then bFound = True
        If K.Borders(wdBorderBottom).LineStyle <> wdLineStyleNone _
          Then bFound = True
        If K.Borders(wdBorderRight).LineStyle <> wdLineStyleNone _
          Then bFound = True

        If bFound Then
            K.Range.Select
            Exit Sub
        End If
    Next k
End Sub
```

Run the macro and it finds and selects the first paragraph that has any border set. The important point to understand here, however, is the use of the For Each loop that is the heart of this macro. Notice the structure of the loop—you specify a variable as a proxy for each element of the collection. In this case, the variable is K and the collection is all the paragraphs in the document. Each time through the loop K is set to a paragraph object within the collection.

Do Loop

One of the most versatile control structures is the Do loop. It allows you to check a condition and then execute a block of code if that condition is met. If the condition isn't met, the block of code is skipped over.

Intrinsic to the Do loop are the While and Until clauses. They modify how the loop works, specifying whether the loop is executed *while* a comparison is true or *until* a comparison is true. Here's a simple example of the loop:

```
Dim J As Integer

J = 0
Do While J < 10
    Selection.TypeText J
    Selection.TypeParagraph
    J = J + 2
Loop
```

This example types the value of J into your document, on its own line. The first time through the loop the value of J is 0, the second time 2, then 4, 6, 8, and finally 10. Once J is incremented to a value of 12, the comparison at the beginning of the loop evaluates as False and the block of code is no longer executed.

This same example could have also been written with the While keyword and comparison at the end of the loop, in this manner:

```
Dim J As Integer

J = 0
Do
    Selection.TypeText J
    Selection.TypeParagraph
    J = J + 2
Loop While J < 10
```

The First Time Through

Given any task utilizing a Do loop there are usually several ways to accomplish it. You can use any of these formats of the loop:

- Do While…Loop
- Do…Loop While
- Do Until…Loop
- Do…Loop Until

Most of the time, you can select the Do loop version that you are most comfortable with and that reads most smoothly to you. You must be aware of one problem, which is exemplified here:

```
Dim X As Integer
Dim Y As Integer
Dim iIncVal As Integer

Do
    MsgBox "X=" & Str(X) & "    Y=" & Str(Y)
    X = X + iIncVal
Loop While X < Y
```

This is a very simple program. If your intent in creating the loop is to print the message box only when X is less than Y, then your logic has failed you. This loop always executes at least once. Instead, use an alternate form of the Do loop:

```
Dim X As Integer
Dim Y As Integer
Dim iIncVal As Integer

Do While X < Y
    MsgBox "X=" & Str(X) & "    Y=" & Str(Y)
    X = X + iIncVal
Loop
```

In this case, the test is done before the loop is entered the first time, and it is never executed if the test fails (when X is greater than or equal to Y).

Exiting a Loop

VBA includes a statement you can use in the middle of your Do loop: Exit Do. If you use an Exit Do in the inner Do loop of a nested set of Do loops, it returns control to the structure one level above. In the following example, when the Exit Do statement is encountered, the next line to be executed is the last Loop statement.

```
Dim sCharBuffer As String
Dim sThisChar As String

Do While Not EOF(FileHandle)
    Input #FileHandle, sCharBuffer
    Do While Len(sCharBuffer) > 0
        sThisChar = Left(sCharBuffer,1)
        sCharBuffer = Right(sCharBuffer, Len(sCharBuffer) - 1)
        If sThisChar = "X" Then
            MsgBox "Found an X in this line"
            Exit Do
        End If
    Loop
Loop
```

Notice the use of Not in the initial Do statement—again for readability. You must not overestimate the importance of making your code easy to follow. A good programmer's source code reads like a story.

While Loops

If you must perform an action over and over until some condition is met, but you don't know how many times it must be done beforehand, you can use a While loop.

In execution, a While loop is identical to a Do While version of a Do loop, as described in the previous section. One advantage of a While loop, however, is that it is syntactically the same construct as is used in several other high-level languages. This makes it more comfortable to use for some people who are new to VBA. Here's a short example of the structure:

```
Dim sResponse As String

sGetResponse                'Get user input
While sResponse <> "Exit"
    ProcessRecord           'Call procedure to process it all
    GetResponse             'Call procedure to get more user input
Wend
```

You need to note that somewhere in your While loop you need to have a way to change the value of whatever you are testing in the loop. If you don't, then the test always returns True and your code remains in an endless loop. In the example above, the GetResponse procedure, called from within the loop, provides a way for the value of sResponse to change.

GoTo

You may have heard many bad things about GoTo. In the early days of BASIC, before the more structured flow control statements you discovered earlier in this chapter were available, GoTo was the easiest way to control program flow. This led to unmanageable code, sometimes called *spaghetti code* because of its similarity to a plate full of snarled spaghetti.

While it has been proven that it is never necessary to use a GoTo statement, it is sometimes convenient to do so. If you don't go overboard with GoTos, their occasional use, in situations that are difficult to solve with other flow control constructs, is considered acceptable programming practice.

Any time you are about to use a GoTo statement, take a few moments to consider whether one of the other program flow constructs can do the job in a more readable fashion. While you may have a good grasp of the overall flow within your program while you are writing it, when you come back to it in a year it takes a while to remember what you were doing. Too many GoTos can make it take far longer.

You can use either a line number or a label with the GoTo statement. Line numbers hearken back to the distant past when BASIC programs required each line to have a line number. VBA doesn't require line numbers, however, so if you use a line number with the GoTo statement, it is treated just like any other label in your program.

Here's how you use the GoTo statement, in general:

```
Dim bStopNow As Boolean

bStopNow = False
...
If bStopNow Then Goto Finished
...
Finished:
End
```

When executed, if bStopNow is changed to True before the If statement is reached, then the GoTo statement transfers execution to the line right after the Finshed label. Note the use of the colon after the label; such colons are not necessary if you use line numbers instead.

Using Data Structures

When dealing with information there is frequently a built-in relationship between certain pieces of that information. For example, a book has a title, an ISBN number, a page count, and an author. Each book has a corresponding value for each of these items. VBA has the capability of using data structures so you can better handle related information.

In this chapter, you learn about the following:

- Data arrays
- User-defined data types
- How to work with data structures

Understanding Arrays

One of the most fundamental data structures is the array. An array is simply an ordered collection of data. Take ten dimes and line them up on the top of a table—you now have an array of dimes. For reference purposes, you can just as easily refer to the first dime in the array or the seventh dime in the array. Arrays are just a way of organizing things that have something in common.

Arrays of related items are used frequently in VBA. The benefit of arrays is that they enable you to categorize items and concentrate only on the element of the array in which you are interested.

When you have an array of similar elements, such as the array of dimes, you have more than just an ordered collection. You know that most aspects of the dimes are identical. All dimes are made of metal and all dimes are of approximately the same diameter, weight, and thickness.

If you collect dimes in the random change you receive each day, there is one thing that is likely to vary from coin to coin—the date of minting. If you were interested in describing your collection of dimes, you may write a list as follows:

- 2004
- 1997
- 2013
- 2008
- 2012
- 2010
- 2007
- 2001
- 1984
- 1949

Each of these ten dates could be an element in an array about your dimes. Each member of the array indicates a different minting year for dimes.

Setting Up an Array

To allocate adequate memory to hold arrays, you must declare the array so that VBA knows how to handle it. One way you can declare the array is to use the Dim statement, as you've seen used quite often through this book. Dim tells VBA to set aside the right amount of space for the array.

Here's the full format for using the Dim statement for arrays:

```
Dim arrayname([lower To ]upper[, [lower To ]upper]...)[As type]
```

In this format *arrayname* is the name of the array, *lower* and *upper* are the lower and upper bounds, respectively, of that array dimension, and *type* is the VBA data type of the array member. For example, you might use either of these to designate your array for dimes:

```
Dim Dimes(101)
Dim Dimes(1 To 101) As Integer
```

Arrays can also be declared Global so they may be accessed in all procedures and modules of your project. The Global statement has the exact same format as the Dim statement. Thus, you'd simply replace Dim with Global in the above examples. Doing so not only declares the array, but also makes it so that the array is universally accessible in your project.

There is one more way in which you can declare an array. You may have an occasion to use an array within a procedure with the requirement that the contents of the array be retained between procedure calls. In other words, you don't want the array to be reinitialized each time you enter the procedure. In these cases, use the Static declaration.

Static is used in the place of Dim when declaring variables in order to retain the value of the declared variable between calls to the procedure. Each Static variable retains its value as long as the program is running.

Changing Arrays on the Fly

Because arrays can consume so much memory it is convenient to change the size of the array as required during run time.

Frequently, you don't know how many dimensions or elements you have until after your program is already running. In these cases, it is also necessary to change the size of the array at run time. The ReDim statement does just that. Here's how you use the statement:

```
ReDim [Preserve ]arrayname ([lower To ]upper[, [lower To ]upper]...)[As
type]
```

When using ReDim, *arrayname* is the name of the array; *lower* and *upper* are the lower and upper bounds, respectively, of that array dimension; and *type* is the data type of the array member.

ReDim reallocates storage space for a previously declared array. The optional Preserve clause causes ReDim to retain the values contained in the array prior to the issue of ReDim. Note that if you use Preserve, you can resize only the last array dimension.

ReDim is used to modify the bounds of an array. In effect, it allows you to dynamically change how your arrays are used while the program is running. You can't use it to change the data type for a variable. For a non-dynamic array, you must get rid of the original variable entirely, and then you are free to redimension the variable.

If you want to free the memory space allocated to a dynamic array, use Erase. When you use Erase, you can get rid of the variable altogether:

```
Erase dimes
```

Multidimensional Arrays

Sometimes there is more than one aspect, or dimension, to an array. In the dimes example, if you look closely, you can also find another feature which varies—the letter on the face of the dime representing the mint at which the dime was made. You can add another column to your list of dime years showing the mint next to the year. You then have a multidimensional array, which you can dimension in the following manner:

```
Dim Dimes(101, 2)
```

Multidimensional arrays are especially useful because they allow you to track and manipulate more than one aspect of the item you have placed into an array. As an example of the usefulness of multidimensional arrays, some of the characteristics of a family have been arranged into an array. This array shows several aspects of each family member:

Name	Sex	Birthday	Age	Occupation
Sam	M	5/8	27	Teacher
Ginger	F	8/11	24	Engineer
Beth	F	12/24	21	Student
Casey	M	6/13	18	Student

To represent the family member array in VBA, you must first declare it. Declaring the array sets aside memory space to hold the array elements. You learned how to do this earlier in the chapter, but you cannot use the Dim statement (by itself) to define an array for your family. The different elements of the array are of different data types. For example, the Name, Sex, and Occupation elements would be strings, while the age and possibly the date element could be expressed as a number. In this case, traditional arrays are all but useless. Instead, you need to learn about user-defined data types (which, conveniently, you'll do later in this chapter).

Getting Information about an Array

Arrays are quite flexible. They can have any number of dimensions, up to whatever your system memory allows. Because arrays are so flexible, VBA provides a way to uncover their bounds. You use the LBound and UBound functions to return the smallest and largest subscript of any array dimension.

```
Dim iHighEnd As Integer
Dim iNumElements As Integer
Dim sRPMArray(99) As String
Dim sBones(499, 3) As String

iHighEnd = UBound(sRPMArray)
iNumElements = UBound(sBones, 2) - LBound(sBones, 2) + 1
```

Starting to Count

You normally start counting at one. Computers and computer languages are typically different, however. VBA starts all of its arrays, unless told otherwise, at zero. You don't have to use the zeroth element if you don't want to; if you do, however, it is available.

Unless you specifically need it, having a zeroth element in all dimensions of all arrays wastes memory. Use the Option Base statement to force VBA to start all array indices from 1 instead of 0, thereby saving valuable memory.

The amount of memory regained depends on the number of dimensions in your arrays. The total memory an array consumes is the product of the number of its dimensions, times the number of elements, multiplied by the number of bytes required for the data type of each element in the array. By reducing the number of elements by one (when you use Option Base 1), you reduce the amount of memory needed to hold the array by the number of dimensions in that array. If your application uses arrays with many dimensions or if it uses many arrays, the savings can be significant.

Using the Option Base statement is optional. If not used, VBA starts all arrays with an index value of 0. If you decide to use Option Base, it must be used in the Declarations section of the project; it must also be used before declaring any arrays. It just requires a simple statement:

```
Option Base 1
```

If an array is declared using the optional To keyword, the array bounds specified with To overrides the bounds set by Option Base. The optional To keyword in the Dim, Global, Static, and ReDim statements provides greater flexibility in the control of array bounds. Its use is recommended.

User-Defined Data Types

Although occasionally you may have related information, the data types often vary. You may, perhaps, want to store information on employees in an array. Each employee has a hire date (Date/Time type), a name (String), a wage rate (Currency), and a job class (Integer). How can you use an array to store this information when the data types vary?

To store the employee information, you must first create a user-defined data type so all elements of the array can be the same. A user-defined data type "packages" a collection of other data types into an "envelope", which can then be treated as though it were a standard VBA data type. Here's an example:

```
Type Employee
    Name As String
    HireDate As Variant
    Dependents(10, 5) As String
End Type
```

The Type statement may only appear in a general code module, and you must place the statement in the Declarations section of the code module. This placement ensures you can use the defined type throughout that module.

The Type statement specifies the name by which this data type will be known—Employee. To obtain the value of one of the variables contained in a user type, use the name of the user type variable and then the name of the specific element in that type, separated by a period. In this way working with user-defined data types is like working with objects:

```
Type Dogs
    Name As String
    Age As Integer
    Breed As String
End Type

Dim PoundDogs(100) As Dogs

PoundDogs(5).Name = "Spot"
PoundDogs(5).Age = 4
PoundDogs(5).Breed = "Scottie"
```

One of the areas where user-defined data types are used quite frequently is with file access, such as when you are working with random-access files. This use of user-defined data types for this purpose is covered in Chapter 14.

Getting Input for Your Macro

The normal way in which Windows prompts a user for input is through the use of a dialog box. The word *dialog* comes from the Greek and means to converse. Dialog boxes are windows that convey information to the user of a program and often allow that user to provide directions back to the computer.

A good example of a dialog box is what you see if you try to exit Word without first saving the changes to your document—the dialog box shown in Figure 9-1 appears. Here you learn what happens next, and then you are given the opportunity to respond to the potential action.

Dialog boxes like these are an integral part of the Windows environment. You can make them a part of your programs as well. VBA provides several functions and facilities for adding and using dialog boxes in your programs. In this chapter, you learn about these capabilities and see examples of how they work.

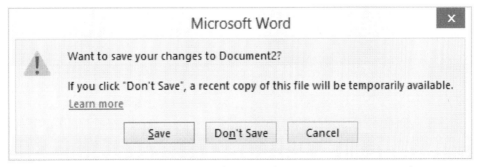

Figure 9-1. *Dialog boxes are used in Windows to communicate with users.*

Creating a Message Box

One of the most useful ways in which Windows programs have evolved in their communication with users is dialog boxes. Before Windows, dialog boxes were the exception rather than the rule. Even today programs written for many other operating systems often don't employ them.

The use of dialog boxes results in cleaner screens because the information to be conveyed or collected doesn't use up valuable space on your screen. You also can use dialog boxes to help guide a user through a specific problem and provide information at just the right moment.

The easiest way to create dialog boxes in VBA is through the use of the MsgBox statement. The MsgBox statement is a flexible means of presenting dialog boxes in which you can change the message, title, and buttons shown; you can even add an optional icon.

The MsgBox statement probably isn't new to you. In fact, it has been used often in the various examples earlier in this book. The format of the statement is easy: You just follow MsgBox with up to three parameters. The first parameter is required; it is a string that indicates what message you want displayed in the message box. The second and third parameters are optional. The second is a numeric value that can indicate what buttons and icons should be displayed, and the third is a string that indicates what title should appear on the dialog box.

There are, in reality, fourth and fifth parameters that you could use. They are optional and aren't used very much at all. (They allow you to specify a help file for the message box and a context in which it operates—esoteric, indeed.) It is the first three that are the most often used, and it is these three that are examined in the following sections.

The Message

The easiest way to use MsgBox is in the form of a statement. All you basically need to do is provide a message you want displayed and VBA takes care of the rest. The dialog box is displayed, along with an OK button for the user to click, as shown in Figure 9-2.

Chapter 9: Getting Input for Your Macro

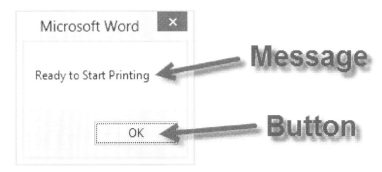

Figure 9-2. *A simple message box consists of a message and an OK button.*

You can add a simple message box like this one to your own program—all it takes is a single statement like this:

```
MsgBox "Ready to Start Printing"
```

Notice three things about this dialog box. First, the title that appears at the top of the dialog box is a default one that lets you know you are running this in Microsoft Word. In the next section you'll discover how to change the title in the dialog box. Second, an OK button is shown in the dialog box, and your program is paused until the user clicks the button. This is the only type of button used for the statement form of MsgBox. How you can use different buttons is covered later in this chapter.

The message you used with the MsgBox statement appears in the message box exactly as you entered it. VBA adjusts the size of the dialog box to compensate for whatever text you enter, and it breaks lines as necessary. For example, consider this code:

```
Dim sTemp As String

sTemp = "This is the message for my custom dialog box and "
sTemp = sTemp & "it is much too long to fit all on one line. "
sTemp = sTemp & "Exactly how long it is depends on when I get "
sTemp = sTemp & "tired of typing. Are you tired of reading yet?"
MsgBox sTemp
```

Note that the code puts together a long message into the sTemp variable. When you run this code, the contents of the sTemp variable are used for the message in the dialog box. What you see is displayed in Figure 9-3.

133

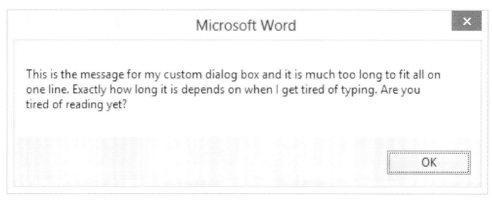

Figure 9-3. The MsgBox function can handle long messages by wrapping them to multiple lines.

Notice that VBA extended the width of the dialog box and wrapped the text to three lines. If you don't like how VBA splits the message over the additional lines, you can control it by adding the vbCrLf (carriage return/line feed) constant in your string where you want the message wrapped. An example of formatting the message in this manner is shown in the following:

```
Dim sTemp As String

sTemp = "This is the message for my custom" & vbCrLf
sTemp = sTemp & "dialog box and it is much too long" & vbCrLf
sTemp = sTemp & "to fit all on one line. Exactly how" & vbCrLf
sTemp = sTemp & "long it is depends on when I get" & vbCrLf
sTemp = sTemp & "tired of typing. Are you tired of" & vbCrLf
sTemp = sTemp & "reading yet?"
MsgBox sTemp
```

When the code is executed, the message in the dialog box (shown in Figure 9-4) is wrapped where you instructed. Notice, as well, that the overall width of the dialog box is narrower than when VBA controls the wrapping.

The Title

The MsgBox statement allows you to change the title of the dialog box as

Figure 9-4. You can control where the message in a MsgBox is wrapped.

well as the message. You can make this change by simply adding another parameter to the statement, as shown in the following code:

```
MsgBox "Ready to Format Your Text",,"Super Formatter 2013"
```

The two commas separating the title from the message are essential. If they are not included, then you get a Type Mismatch error when you try to execute this statement. Normally, a value indicating a type of message box is added between the commas. These values are discussed more fully in the following section.

Icons, Buttons, and Responses

Much of the flexibility of the MsgBox statement is provided through the use of the second parameter. It determines which icons and buttons are shown in the dialog box.

Changing Icons

VBA allows you to use any of four different icons in your message boxes. These icons are rather standard for Windows dialog boxes; they seem to be used in virtually every program you can think of. You indicate an icon by using a numeric value—or a VBA enumeration equivalent to the numeric value—for the second parameter. Here are the values you can use, along with their meanings:

- 16 or vbCritical (stop sign)
- 32 or vbQuestion (question mark)
- 48 or vbExclamation (exclamation mark)
- 64 or vbInformation ("i" for information)

Use the stop sign for serious errors or situations that can cause the loss of data. Use the question mark when obtaining answers to routine questions. The exclamation point is for situations that may have been unexpected by the user, or for emphasis of a message. Use the "i" when presenting a message purely for informational purposes.

As an example, try out the following program code:

```
Dim sMessage As String
Dim sTitle As String

sMessage = "You just eliminated the national debt" & vbCrLf
sMessage = sMessage & "and established world peace."
sTitle = "Acme Problem Solver"
MsgBox sMessage, vbInformation, sTitle
```

When you run the code, you see a message box that looks like what you see in Figure 9-5.

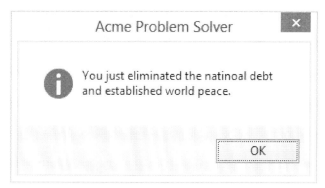

Figure 9-5. *VBA allows you to modify the icon displayed in a message box.*

Changing Buttons

Besides allowing you to add icons to your message boxes, VBA allows you to change which buttons are displayed at the bottom of the box. There are six different buttons that you can use:

- 0 or vbOKOnly (OK button)
- 1 or vbOKCancel (OK and Cancel buttons)
- 2 or vbAbortRetryIgnore (Abort, Retry, and Ignore buttons)
- 3 or vbYesNoCancel (Yes, No, and Cancel buttons)
- 4 or vbYesNo (Yes and No buttons)
- 5 or vbRetryCancel (Retry and Cancel buttons)

Changing buttons in the dialog box is just as easy as adding icons. As an example, the following code would display a standard message box, but with Yes and No buttons at the bottom:

```
Dim sMessage As String
Dim sTitle As String

sMessage = "Do you want your program to work?"
sTitle = "Acme Program Fixer"
MsgBox sMessage, vbYesNo, sTitle
```

Combining Buttons and Icons

VBA allows you to combine both the icon type values and the button type values so that you can display both icons and different buttons in your dialog boxes. All you need to do is add the two values together.

For example, the value to display a stop sign icon is 16 (or vbCritical) and the value to display Yes, No, and Cancel buttons is 3 (or vbYesNoCancel). To display them both, you would use a type value of 16 + 3, or 19, in your program. Here's an example of how that works in your program code:

```
Dim sMessage As String
Dim sTitle As String

sMessage = "What should we do with the boss today?"
sTitle = "Company Relations"
MsgBox sMessage, vbQuestion + vbAbortRetryIgnore, sTitle
```

Note how the constants for the icon (vbQuestion) and the buttons (vbAbortRetryIgnore) are added together. The result is what is displayed in Figure 9-6.

Figure 9-6. You can combine icons and buttons in a single message box.

User Feedback

It doesn't usually make sense to change the buttons being displayed in a message box if using them has no effect. So far you have done nothing but use the MsgBox statement, which simply displays the message box and then returns to your program. VBA provides a function version of MsgBox that allows you to determine which button the user selected. Based on this information, you can then take the appropriate action.

The biggest difference between using MsgBox as a statement and as a function is that when you are using it as a function, you enclose the parameters in parentheses. You also provide a variable into which the return value from the message box is stored. Here's an example:

```
Dim sMessage As String
Dim sTitle As String
Dim iYesNo As Integer

sMessage = "Do you want to proceed?"
sTitle = "Last Chance to Quit"
iYesNo = MsgBox(sMessage, vbQuestion+vbYesNo, sTitle)
```

You should note that the only difference between the MsgBox statement and function is that the function is used to return a value indicating which button the user pressed. After the MsgBox function has been invoked and the user has selected a button, the value returned ranges from 1 to 7, and corresponds to one of these seven possible buttons:

- 1 or vbOK (OK button was clicked)
- 2 or vbCancel (Cancel button was clicked)
- 3 or vbAbort (Abort button was clicked)
- 4 or vbRetry (Retry button was clicked)
- 5 or vbIgnore (Ignore button was clicked)
- 6 or vbYes (Yes button was clicked)
- 7 or vbNo (No button was clicked)

You can then make a determination of what to do based on the result. Many times programs use the Select Case construct (see Chapter 7) to take action after returning from a message box.

Getting User Input

A message box is great as long as you need only one of seven answers. What if you need more input? For example, what if you need to know a date to use when creating a new document? When you need more input it is best to use the InputBox function. This function allows you to get a text string from the user and assign it to a variable.

The simplest use of the InputBox function is to specify a message you want to appear in the box, like this:

```
sRawInput = InputBox("Enter your name?")
```

This results in a simple dialog box like what is shown in Figure 9-7. Note that the message is displayed near the top of the dialog box.

The InputBox function allows quite a few more parameters than just a prompt message, however. There are actually seven different parameters that are possible with the function, although it is only the first five that most people use. (The sixth and seventh parameters allow you to specify a help file for the input box and a context in which it operates. These are too advanced for the common uses of InputBox.) Each of the common InputBox parameters is examined in the following sections.

Remember that the InputBox function is designed to get input from the user. It contains only two buttons, as shown in Figure 9-7. If the OK button is clicked (or the **Enter** key is pressed), then a string value of what was entered in the dialog box, by the user, is returned. If the Cancel button is clicked (or the **Esc** key is pressed), then an empty string is returned.

The Prompt

As with MsgBox, whatever message you use with InputBox appears on-screen exactly as you type it. You are limited, however, to messages that are approximately 1024 characters long. Attempting to use a longer message results in a program error, but come on—if you can't get your message across in over a thousand characters, something may be wrong with your message!

If the message you enter is too long to fit on a single line, VBA wraps it automatically to the next line. If you want to make your message wrap at

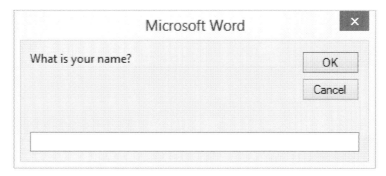

Figure 9-7. An input box can be a very simple way to get user input.

specific places, you can use the vbCrLf constant within the string, just as you can with the MsgBox statement.

The Title

Normally the InputBox function simply displays a title that lets you know you are working in Microsoft Word (see Figure 9-7). You can, however, display a title more to your liking by adding another parameter to the input box function. Use the code shown in Listing 8.11 to generate a dialog box with a custom title and message, as shown in Figure 9-8.

```
Dim sMessage As String
Dim sTitle As String
Dim sRawInput As String

sMessage = "Enter the name you want" & vbCrLf
sMessage = sMessage & "used for the document."
sTitle = "Nifty Document Creator"
sRawInput = InputBox(sMessage, sTitle)
```

Default Input

By adding a third parameter to the InputBox function, VBA allows you to indicate default text that can be used in your input box. This text is displayed in the text box at the bottom of the dialog box, and the user can accept it by simply pressing ENTER or clicking OK. Conversely, if the user starts typing right away, the default is erased and replaced with whatever the user is typing.

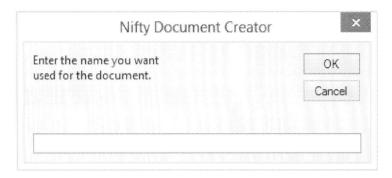

Figure 9-8. *You can specify a title for an input box.*

As an example, the following code uses today's date as a default to the prompt. Note that the default should be a string value; in this case it is created using the Format function, as described in Chapter 6.

```
Dim sMessage As String
Dim sTitle As String
Dim sDefault As String
Dim sRawInput As String

sMessage = "What date do you want used for the document?"
sTitle = "Nifty Document Creator"
sDefault = Format(Now,"MM/DD/YYYY")
sRawInput = InputBox(sMessage, sTitle, sDefault)
```

Screen Coordinates

The fourth and fifth parameters that you can use with the InputBox function allow you to specify where, on the screen, the dialog box should be displayed. These parameters must be used as a pair; they designate the x and y coordinates of the upper-left corner of the input box.

You need to specify the position coordinates in a unit of measure known as *twips*, which are approximately 1/1440 of an inch. If specific screen coordinates are omitted, the dialog box is centered from left to right and appears about one-third down the screen from top to bottom.

Built-In Dialog Boxes

You probably noticed that Word includes quite a few dialog boxes that spring into action at various times. These dialog boxes are the primary method that you use to configure how the program works or specify what you want it to do.

When it comes to VBA macros, Word makes the vast majority of its dialog box available in the Dialogs collection. Since each dialog box is different, how you use them in your macro depends not only on what you want to do but on which dialog box you are working with. The following sections examine which dialog boxes are available and how you work with them.

Available Dialog Boxes

Word uses dialog boxes—lots of dialog boxes. At last count, there were over 230 different dialog boxes that belong to the Dialogs collection. With that many dialog boxes, it can be hard to locate the one you want to use.

The easiest way to access a dialog box is simply to include its name within the parentheses of the collection, as shown here:

```
Dialogs(wdDialogFileNew)
```

The problem is figuring out what names that Word has assigned to the various dialog boxes. (This name is what you include in the parentheses.) With over 230 dialog boxes available, finding the names is no small task. Here's the easiest way to find them out:

1. Press **Alt+F11** to display the Visual Basic Editor.
2. Press **F2** to display the Object Browser.
3. Using the Project/Library drop-down list, choose Word.
4. In the Classes list, choose <globals>. This should be the first option in the list. The Object Browser now appears as shown in Figure 9-9.
5. Scroll through the Members of <globals> list until you locate the names for the dialog boxes.

The list of global names presented in the Object Browser is very long, but they aren't all names for dialog boxes. You'll know when you get to the appropriate names when you find those that begin with the characters *wdDialog*.

How Word determines the dialog box name is rooted in history—it depends on the old (pre-Word 2007) menu name and the command name on that menu. Thus, if you are looking for the dialog box that allows you to create a new document, the proper name is wdDialogFileNew, as noted earlier in this section. The *wdDialog* is standard to all names, and *FileNew* refers to the old menu (File) and the command on that menu (New).

If you prefer, you can find a list of Word 2007 dialog box names at this address:

```
http://msdn.microsoft.com/en-us/library/bb214033.aspx
```

Chapter 9: Getting Input for Your Macro

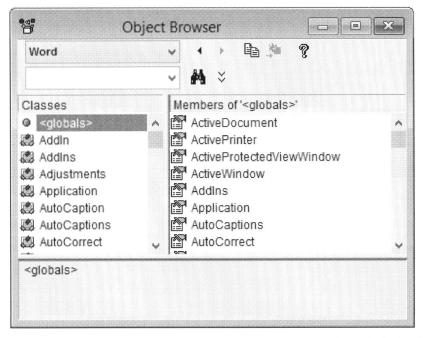

Figure 9-9. *Finding the names for all of Word's dialog boxes takes a little sleuthing.*

You can find a list of Word 2010 dialog box names at this address:

`http://msdn.microsoft.com/en-us/library/ff836540%28v=office.14%29.aspx`

Finally, you can find a list of Word 2013 dialog box names at this address:

`http://msdn.microsoft.com/en-us/library/ff836540%28v=office.15%29.aspx`

Displaying Dialog Boxes

Displaying a built-in dialog box is easy to do—all you need to do is use the Show method. For instance, if you want to display the Open dialog box, you could use the following code:

`Dialogs(wdDialogFileOpen).Show`

With the dialog box displayed, your macro waits for the user to take some action that results in the dialog box being closed. Once that is done, then your macro continues on its way.

Of course, you may not want your macro to continue blindly on its way after a dialog box is closed. Instead, you may want to get some feedback as to *how* the user closed the dialog box. This is done by checking what value is returned by the Show method. For instance, the following code is used to determine if the dialog box was closed by clicking Cancel:

```
Dim iRetVal As Integer

iRetVal = Dialogs(wdDialogFileOpen).Show
If iRetVal = 0 Then
    MsgBox "You didn't pick a file!"
End If
```

The values that can be returned by the Show method are as follows:

- **-2**. The Close button was clicked.
- **-1**. The OK button or its equivalent (such as Open) was clicked.
- **0**. The Cancel button was clicked.
- **>0**. A command button where 1 is the first button, 2 is the second button, and so on.

If you want to take actions based on what button was clicked in a dialog box, you'll need to play around a bit and do some testing to see what is returned by the particular dialog box you are working with.

Accessing Dialog Box Settings

If your macro couldn't access the information available in a dialog box, then the versatility of working with dialog boxes would be very much diminished. Fortunately, VBA allows you to access many of the various settings on dialog boxes. You access these by examining the properties that Word makes available for the dialog box. These properties correspond with the settings for various controls in the dialog box.

As an example, let's say that you wanted to find out the name of the printer driver that is currently being used. You can use the following code line:

```
MsgBox Dialogs(wdDialogFilePrintSetup).Printer
```

This works because the Printer property is available for access in the Print Setup dialog box.

The easiest way to determine what properties Word makes available for each dialog box is to look at the detailed documentation. This is available at the Microsoft websites referenced earlier; these are for Word 2007, Word 2010, and Word 2013, respectively:

```
http://msdn.microsoft.com/en-us/library/bb214033.aspx
http://msdn.microsoft.com/en-us/library/ff836540%28v=office.14%29.aspx
http://msdn.microsoft.com/en-us/library/ff836540%28v=office.15%29.aspx
```

Each list shows the dialog box names and, in the third column, which properties you can access on each of those dialog boxes.

10

Working with a Document

At the heart of everything that Word does is the document. We tend to take documents for granted, but everything created in Word is contained within one. Because they are at the heart of Word, they are also at the heart of working with VBA in Word. In this chapter you'll discover all sorts of things about documents:

- How to create new documents
- How you can open existing documents
- Getting a document's name
- The power in working with Paragraph objects
- How to access style information
- How to work with bookmarks

The Document Object

A Document object represents, well, a single document open in Word at the current time. Each Document object is part of the Documents collection. Word allows you to have open, at any given time, any number of documents, so the Documents collection can contain any number of Document objects.

Individual Document objects can be accessed in two ways. First, you can access them by index or by name within the Documents collection; this access method is no different than any other collection you may work with. This means that you can use a loop to step through the collection and access each Document's information, like this:

```
Dim d As Document
Dim sDocNames(99) As String
Dim iNumDocs As Integer

iNumDocs = 0
For Each d in Documents
    iNumDocs = iNumDocs + 1
    sDocNames(iNumDocs) = d.Name
Next d
```

When this code is through, the sDocNames array contains the names of all the documents currently open in Word. (You'll learn more about document names later in this chapter.) The key here is to notice how easy it is to access information about the individual documents simply by accessing each member of the Documents collection.

The second way to access an individual Document object is with the special ActiveDocument object. This object is synonymous with whichever document currently is active (has focus) in Word. The actual Document object to which it refers changes as the selected document changes. It is a very handy object, one that you'll use many times in your macros.

There are dozens of methods and properties that belong to Document objects, but only a few of them are key to successfully working with those objects.

Creating New Documents

It is often necessary to create new documents in a macro. Perhaps you need to create some information and you don't want that information to be inserted in the existing document. The answer is to use the Add method with the Documents collection:

```
Documents.Add
```

This usage creates a new document using the Normal template and adds the Document object to the Documents collection. When you add a new document, you now have a minimum of two documents open in Word—the one that existed when you ran your macro and the one you just added. Because of this, it is helpful to be able to keep track of which document you are working with in your macro.

A common technique for doing this is to assign the Document objects to your own object variables. Consider the following code:

```
Dim docThis As Document
Dim docThat As Document

Set docThis = ActiveDocument
Documents.Add
Set docThat = ActiveDocument
docThis.Activate
```

Note that the Set keyword, discussed in Chapter 2, is used to make the docThis variable equal to the ActiveDocument object. The ActiveDocument object is a special instance of whatever document Word considers active at the current time; it is whatever document currently has the focus.

The code then uses the Add method to add a document, just as you learned. When this occurs, the new document then has focus as far as Word is concerned. That is why the next line also sets the docThat variable equal to the ActiveDocument. The final line activates the original document, represented by the docThis variable; it gives focus back to the original document.

What you end up with when executing this code is docThis being equivalent to the first document and docThat being equivalent to the newly added document. You can then reference each document in your code directly using the object variables, docThis and docThat.

Opening Existing Documents

If your macro needs to open an existing document, you use the Open method with the Documents collection. If the method is successful in opening the document, then a Document object is added to the collection and refers to the document you opened.

Here is how you open a document:

```
Documents.Open("c:/document/mydoc.docx")
```

The important thing to keep in mind here is that in order to be unambiguous the filename must include the full path to the document. If you don't include the full path, there is a greater chance that VBA won't be successful in opening the file because you never really know what directory the program considers the current directory.

In all of its glory, the Open method allows you to specify up to 16 parameters. All of these are optional, with the exception of the first parameter, the filename. The other 15 parameters are as follows, in order:

- **ConfirmConversions.** Defaults to True, but can be set to False to hide the Convert File dialog box if the file is not in Microsoft Word format.
- **ReadOnly.** True or False, depending on whether you want the document opened as read-only or not. Setting the parameter to False does not override the Read-Only Recommended setting if the document was saved with it.
- **AddToRecentFiles.** Defaults to True, adding the document to the MRI list in Word.
- **PasswordDocument.** The document's password.
- **PasswordTemplate.** The password for the document's template.
- **Revert.** If set to True, causes a currently open document with the same name to revert to whatever is stored in the file. If set to False, then the already-open document is activated.
- **WritePasswordDocument.** The password for saving document changes.
- **WritePasswordTemplate.** The password for saving changes in the document's template.
- **Format.** Which file converter should be used to open the document. Defaults to Word figuring out which converter is best, if one is necessary. If you want to set this parameter to a specific format, you'll want to visit VBA's online help system.
- **Encoding.** The document encoding to be used to view the document. If you want to set the encoding, then you'll again want to visit the online help system.

- **Visible.** True or False, depending on whether you want the document to be visible after opening.

- **OpenConflictDocument.** True or False, depending on whether you want a conflict file opened for the document if it has a conflict with an offline document.

- **OpenAndRepair.** True or False depending on whether you want Word to try to repair the document if it detects any corruption within it.

- **DocumentDirection.** Specifies whether the document reads left-to-right or right-to-left. Only has meaning in those languages that read right-to-left.

- **NoEncodingDialog.** True of False depending on whether you want the Encoding dialog box displayed if Word cannot recognize the encoding scheme used for the document.

Of course, most of these parameters you would never use in opening a plain old Word document. In most cases you can get by just fine with using just the filename and its path.

Getting to a Document's Name

One of the properties associated with a document allows you to determine what its name is. This is handy when you are working with whatever document the user opened before your macro started running.

In reality, there are three properties that are related to names:

- **Name.** Returns the name of the document, meaning the filename the document uses when saved on disk. If the document has yet to be saved, then a placeholder name (such as Document1 or Document2) is returned.

- **FullName.** Returns the full path and filename for the document. If the document has yet to be saved, then this property returns the same as the Name property.

- **Path.** Returns the full path to the folder in which the filename is stored, without a trailing slash.

In looking at the properties related to document names, you may wonder how you can really tell whether a document has been previously saved or not. You'll note that the Name property returns a placeholder name if the document has not been saved, but there is nothing to stop the user from saving a document using that placeholder name.

The technique to use is to compare the Name property to the FullName property. If they are the same, then the document has never been saved:

```
Dim bSavedBefore As Boolean

bSavedBefore = True
With ActiveDocument
    If .Name = .FullName Then bSavedBefore = False
End With
If bSavedBefore Then
    MsgBox "Document has been saved before."
Else
    MsgBox "Document has not been saved yet."
End If
```

Accessing Paragraphs

Perhaps the most important object in a document is the Paragraph object. The Word object model includes a Paragraphs collection which consists of all the paragraphs in a document. It is important because by understanding how to access the Paragraph objects in a macro, you can step through each paragraph of a document and make changes in almost any way you desire.

Adding Paragraphs

In Chapter 11 you discover how you can use the Selection object to add text to your documents. You can also add text by manipulating the Paragraphs collection for a document. Consider the following code line:

```
ActiveDocument.Paragraphs.Add
```

This does nothing more than add a new paragraph at the end of the document. Once added, you can then manipulate the paragraph in any way you desire, including adding text to the paragraph.

For instance, let's say you wanted to add seven new paragraphs to your document and you want each new paragraph to contain text that is equal to the day of the week. You could use this code:

```
Dim J As Integer
Dim iCount As Integer

iCount = ActiveDocument.Paragraphs.Count
For J = 1 To 7
    ActiveDocument.Paragraphs.Add
    ActiveDocument.Paragraphs(iCount + J).Range.Text = WeekdayName(J)
Next J
```

This code adds the seven paragraphs and sets the text of those paragraphs to be the weekday names, Sunday through Saturday. (The WeekdayName function is described in Chapter 6.)

Accessing Paragraphs

A more powerful use of the Paragraphs collection is the ability to step through the text of each paragraph and make decisions based upon what is found in the text. You can access the text in a particular paragraph by just looking at the Text property of the Paragraph object's Range, in this manner:

```
sRawText = ActiveDocument.Paragraphs(3).Range.Text
```

After this code is executed, sRawText contains all the text that was in the third paragraph of the document. Combining this capability with a For Each loop, you could step through a document and make changes in the paragraph text, in this manner:

```
Dim p As Paragraph
Dim sRaw As String
Dim bChanged As Boolean

For Each p In ActiveDocument.Paragraphs
    sRaw = p.Range.Text
    bChanged = False
    While InStr(sRaw, Chr(151))
        sRaw = Replace(sRaw, Chr(151), "&mdash;")
        bChanged = True
    Wend
    If bChanged Then p.Range.Text = sRaw
Next p
```

This code steps through each paragraph of the document and, if it finds an em-dash (the character code for an em-dash is 151), it replaces it with the HTML equivalent for the character. If the paragraph's text is changed, then the routine stuffs the modified text back into the paragraph.

You should note that this method of processing text is great if you don't really care about any explicit formatting that the user has applied to the text in the paragraph. When you stuff the text back into the paragraph, it is stuffed in without any formatting at all; it is similar to selecting the text and pressing **CTRL+SPACEBAR** to reset the formatting to whatever the formatting of the underlying paragraph style dictates.

Deleting Paragraphs

Just as you can delete objects from most other collections, you can also delete them from the Paragraphs collection. It isn't as straightforward as it is with other collections, however, since the there is no Delete method for the Paragraphs collection. Instead, you must address each member of the collection as a Range object and then delete that object.

Here's an example that shows how to delete paragraphs:

```
Dim iPNum As Integer
Dim J As Integer

iPNum = ActiveDocument.Paragraphs.Count \ 5
iPNum = iPNum * 5

For J = iPNum To 1 Step -5
    ActiveDocument.Paragraphs(J).Range.Delete
Next J
```

This code first looks at how many paragraphs there are in the document and then determines the largest multiple of 5 in that count. Thus, if there are 57 paragraphs in the document, then the largest multiple of 5 is 55. The loop within the code starts with this largest multiple and counts downward in increments of 5. Each fifth paragraph is thereby deleted from the document.

Accessing Styles

Since styles underlie all of Word's formatting, each paragraph in a document has a style associated with it. This style can be accessed by looking at the Style property, in this manner:

```
sStyleName = ActiveDocument.Paragraphs(J).Style
```

You can change the style assigned to a paragraph by simply changing the name of the Style property used with a paragraph. For instance, you might want to change all instances of the Heading 1 style to Heading 2. This can be done in this manner:

```
Dim p As Paragraph

For Each p In ActiveDocument.Paragraphs
    If p.Style = "Heading 1" Then
        p.Style = "Heading 2"
    End If
Next p
```

This brings to light a very important point—did you notice how easy it was to change the style of a paragraph? All you need to do is change the name of the Style property to a valid style name, and Word obligingly reformats the paragraph using that style.

VBA also allows you to take actions based upon the style of particular paragraphs. For instance, you could easily develop a macro that pulls all the headings in a document off to a new document:

```
Sub MoveHeadings()
    Dim docThis As Document
    Dim docThat As Document
    Dim p As Paragraph

    Set docThis = ActiveDocument
    Documents.Add
    Set docThat = ActiveDocument

    For Each p in docThis.Paragraphs
        If Left(p.Style,7) = "Heading" Then
            J = docThat.Paragraphs.Count
            docThat.Paragraphs(J).Range.Text = p.Range.Text
```

```
            docThat.Paragraphs(J).Style = p.Style
        End If
    Next p
End Sub
```

This macro creates a new document and then examines each paragraph in the original document. If it finds any paragraphs formatted with a heading style (Heading 1, Heading 2, etc.) then it transfers the paragraph to the new document and formats it with the appropriate style. Nothing in the original document is affected and you end up with a "clean" outline in the new document.

Using Explicit Formatting

Styles aren't the only way to apply formatting within a document. Everyone knows that as you are using Word you can apply formatting to paragraphs by using some of the tools on both the Home and Page Layout tabs of the ribbon, and additional paragraph formatting tools are contained in the Paragraph dialog box. Explicitly formatting individual characters is done by using some of the formatting tools on the Home tab of the ribbon and in the Font dialog box. All in all, there are dozens and dozens of tools and settings you can use to make your paragraphs and characters look "just right."

Word's object model gives VBA complete access to all of those formatting tools. You can easily adjust both paragraph and character formatting using those tools.

Formatting Paragraphs

To key to explicitly formatting paragraphs is to use the ParagraphFormat object. This is a child of the Range object for an individual paragraph. (Ranges are described more fully in Chapter 11.) Essentially the ParagraphFormat object represents a set of formatting settings that can be applied to an individual paragraph.

The ParagraphFormat object has quite a few properties associated with it. The purpose of these properties is reflected in their names. Here are the ones you'll access most often:

- **Alignment.** Controls the alignment of the paragraph. Most common settings are specified with the following Word enumerations: wdAlignParagraphCenter, wdAlignParagraphDistribute, wdAlignParagraphJustify, wdAlignParagraphLeft, or wdAlignParagraphRight.
- **BaseLineAlignment.** Controls how the fonts in the paragraph are aligned in relation to the font's baseline.
- **Borders.** Returns a Borders collection that contains all the Border objects associated with the paragraph.
- **Duplicate.** Returns a copy of the current ParagraphFormat object.
- **FirstLineIndent.** Specifies the distance, in points, that the first line is indented from the LeftIndent property.
- **Hyphenation.** True or False, indicating whether the paragraph is to be automatically hyphenated.
- **KeepTogether.** True or False, indicating whether the paragraph should remain together on the same page.
- **KeepWithNext.** True or False, indicating whether the paragraph should stay on the same page as the next paragraph.
- **LeftIndent.** Specifies the distance, in points, that the paragraph is indented from the left margin.
- **LineSpacing.** Specifies the line spacing for the paragraph, in points.
- **LineSpacingRule.** Specifies the line spacing model for the paragraph.
- **LineUnitAfter.** Specifies the amount of spacing, in gridlines, after the paragraph.
- **LineUnitBefore.** Specifies the amount of spacing, in gridlines, before the paragraph.
- **MirrorIndents.** True, False, or wdUndefined, indicating whether the LeftIndent and RightIndent margins are equal.
- **NoLineNumber.** True or False, indicating whether line numbers are turned off for the paragraph.
- **OutlineLevel.** Specifies the outline level associated with the paragraph.
- **PageBreakBefore.** True or False, indicating whether Word should place an automatic page break before the paragraph.

- **RightIndent.** Specifies the distance, in points, that the paragraph is indented from the right margin.
- **Shading.** Returns a Shading object that defines the shading applied to the paragraph.
- **SpaceAfter.** Specifies the amount of spacing, in points, after the paragraph.
- **SpaceBefore.** Specifies the amount of spacing, in points, before the paragraph.
- **SpaceBeforeAuto.** True or False, indicating if Word should automatically set the amount of space before the paragraph.
- **Style.** Name of the paragraph style applied to the paragraph.
- **TabStops.** Returns a TabStops collection that contains individual TabStop objects defining the tabs set for the paragraph.
- **TextboxTightWrap.** Specifies how tightly text wraps around shapes or text boxes.
- **WidowControl.** True or False, indicating if the first and last lines of the paragraph remain on the same page as the next and previous lines when paginating the document.

There are a few more properties associated with ParagraphFormat objects, but they generally have to do with foreign-language versions of Word or are so esoteric that they are seldom used.

As an example of how to use the ParagraphFormat object, you may want to change the formatting of a specific paragraph in your document. Let's say that you want to change the fifth paragraph in the document so that it is justified and uses 18-point line spacing. You could do this in this way:

```
With ActiveDocument.Paragraphs(5).Range.ParagraphFormat
    .Alignment = wdAlignParagraphJustify
    .LineSpacingRule = wdLineSpaceAtLeast
    .LineSpacing = 18
    .KeepTogether = True
End With
```

The interesting thing is that you can create an independent ParagraphFormat object that defines how you want a paragraph to look, and then apply that object to existing paragraphs in the document. This might sound like a way to create styles, but it actually is a way to mix styles with explicit formatting. (Remember that the ParagraphFormat object has a Style property, as well.)

For example, let's say that you have a base style of Heading 1, but you want a few paragraphs in your document to vary from that style slightly. You can do this by defining a ParagraphFormat object and applying it to the desired paragraphs:

```
Dim oMyPar As ParagraphFormat

Set oMyPar = New ParagraphFormat
With oMyPar
    .Alignment = wdAlignParagraphCenter
    .KeepTogether = True
    .KeepWithNext = True
    .SpaceBefore = 144
End With

ActiveDocument.Paragraphs(5).Style = "Heading 1"
ActiveDocument.Paragraphs(5).Range.ParagraphFormat = oMyPar
```

Note that the code creates a new object variable, oMyPar, which is a ParagraphFormat. It then sets some properties that define how you want the paragraph formatted. The Heading 1 style is then applied to the target paragraph, which in this instance is the fifth paragraph. Finally, the variations are applied to the same paragraph simply by applying the oMyPar variable. You could easily accomplish the same task on any number of paragraphs in the document.

Earlier in this section you learned that a ParagraphFormat object includes a Style property. That may make you question why the Heading 1 style, in this example, needed to be applied separately to the target paragraph. The answer is simple—if you try to set the Style property for a stand-alone ParagraphFormat object (such as oMyPar), then VBA generates an error; it won't let you assign that property when working with the object created in that way.

Formatting Characters

Word also allows you to assign formatting to specific characters. This is done using the Font object, which has quite a few properties associated with it.

These define all the various permutations of how a character can appear. Here are the most-used properties for the Font object:

- **AllCaps.** True or False, indicating if the characters should be shown as uppercase.
- **Bold.** True or False, indicating if the characters are bold.
- **Borders.** Returns a Borders collection that contains all the Border objects associated with the character.
- **ColorIndex.** Specifies the color for the characters.
- **DoubleStrikeThrough.** True or False, indicating whether there is a double strikethrough on the characters.
- **Emboss.** True or False, indicating if the character appears embossed.
- **Engrave.** True or False, indicating if the character appears engraved.
- **Hidden.** True or False, indicating if the character is hidden.
- **Italic.** True or False, indicating if the characters are italic.
- **Kerning.** Specifies the minimum font size for which Word performs kerning.
- **Name.** Specifies the name of the font.
- **Outline.** True or False, indicating if the character appears as an outline.
- **Position.** Specifies the vertical position of the character, in points, relative to the baseline.
- **Scaling.** Specifies the scaling percentage for the character.
- **Shading.** Returns a Shading object that defines the shading applied to the character.
- **Shadow.** True or False, indicating if the character appears shadowed.
- **Size.** Specifies the size of the font, in points.
- **SmallCaps.** True or False, indicating if the characters should be shown as small uppercase letters.
- **Spacing.** Specifies the spacing between characters, in points.
- **StrikeThrough.** True or False, indicating whether there is a single strikethrough on the characters.

- **Subscript.** True or False, indicating if the character should be displayed below the baseline and smaller.
- **Superscript.** True or False, indicating if the character should be displayed above the baseline and smaller.
- **TextColor.** Returns a ColorFormat object that defines the color for the character.
- **TextShadow.** Returns a ShadowFormat object that defines the formatting for the character's shadow.
- **Underline.** Specifies the type of underline for the character.
- **UnderlineColor.** Specifies the color of the underline.

There are other properties that are associated with the Font object, but they are very esoteric or associated with foreign-language implementations of Word. These properties are the ones you'll find yourself using the most often.

To use the Font object to affect the formatting of some text, you could use it to affect the formatting of whatever word (or words) you've selected:

```
With Selection.Font
    .Bold = True
    .Italic = True
    .ColorIndex = wdRed
    .Size = 16
End With
```

The code makes the selected text red, bold, and italic. It also increases the size of the typeface to 16 points without changing the typeface itself. (How you use the Selection object is described in more detail in Chapter 11.)

Using Bookmarks

One of the most common elements in a Word document is a bookmark. Actually, there could be dozens or scores of bookmarks in a document, each referring to either a single location or pieces of selected text. Each bookmark that you create in a document, whether manually or with a macro, is part of the Bookmarks collection. Each document has a Bookmarks collection and each selection or range can have its own Bookmarks collection which is a subset of the Bookmarks collection associated with the document in which the selection or range is located. (Selections and ranges are discussed more fully in Chapter 11.)

Since bookmarks are such a big part of Word documents, you need to understand how to work with them.

Adding Bookmarks

Earlier in this chapter you discovered that you can use the Add method to create a new document. Bookmarks are very similar in this regard—you use the Add method to create a new bookmark. For instance, if you want to add a bookmark that refers to whatever the user has selected in the document, you can use this code:

```
ActiveDocument.Bookmarks.Add "ThisPlace", Selection.Range
```

Don't worry about the Selection.Range terminology right now; you'll discover more about selections and ranges in Chapter 11. The important thing is to understand that this code results in a bookmark being added to the current document, that it uses the name *ThisPlace,* and that it is equal to whatever is selected in the document. You can see that the bookmark is added by displaying the Insert tab of the ribbon and clicking the Bookmark tool in the Links group.

If the bookmark name you specify in the code ("ThisPlace") is a duplicate of a bookmark already in the document, then VBA replaces the existing bookmark with this new definition. It does this without warning, which makes the Add method just a bit dangerous. If you want to check to see whether a bookmark with a particular name already exists, then you'll want to use the Exists method:

```
ActiveDocument.Bookmarks.Exists("ThisPlace")
```

This method returns True or False depending on whether the bookmark exists or not. Using this method you can develop a technique that allows your macro to always save a bookmark using a unique name:

```
Dim sBMName As String
Dim J As Integer

J = 0
sBMName = "MyBkMk" & Format(J,"0000")
Do Until Not ActiveDocument.Bookmarks.Exists(sBMName)
    J = J + 1
    sBMName = "MyBkMk" & Format(J,"0000")
Loop
ActiveDocument.Bookmarks.Add sBMName, Selection.Range
MsgBox "Bookmark named " & sBMName & " added"
Dialogs(wdDialogInsertBookmark).Show
```

This code handles up to 10,000 unique bookmark names, numbered MyBkMk0000 through MyBkMk9999. It simply checks to see, in order, if a name exists. When it completes the Do loop a unique bookmark name is ensured. The bookmark is then added, a message box to that effect is displayed, and finally the Bookmarks dialog box is displayed.

Accessing Existing Bookmarks

You access individual bookmarks by pulling them out of the collection to which they belong. Thus, an individual bookmark in a collection can be accessed by either an index value or by a name. This is exemplified in these lines of code:

```
Dim BkMk1 As Bookmark
Dim BkMk2 As Bookmark

Set BkMk1 = ActiveDocument.Bookmarks(2)
Set BkMk2 = ActiveDocument.Bookmarks("ThisPlace")
```

The first line of code sets the BkMk1 object equal to the second bookmark in the collection, while the second line of code sets the BkMk2 object equal to the bookmark named ThisPlace.

If you want to select a particular bookmark in the document then you can use the Select method, as follows:

```
ActiveDocument.Bookmarks("MyBookmark").Select
BkMk1.Select
```

The second usage assumes that you previously set BkMk1 equal to an existing Bookmark object.

Individual bookmarks can mark either a text selection in a document or it can mark a single location. You can determine whether a bookmark represents text or a location by looking at the Empty property. If the property is True, then the bookmark is a location only. If it is more than a location, then Empty is False.

To show how you can access all your bookmarks in a meaningful way, consider the following macro:

```
Sub CreateBkMkList()
    Dim docThis As Document
    Dim J As Integer

    Set docThis = ActiveDocument
    Documents.Add

    Selection.TypeText "The following are bookmarks that mark "
    Selection.TypeText "text selections"
    Selection.TypeParagraph

    For J = 1 To docThis.Bookmarks.Count
        If Not docThis.Bookmarks(J).Empty Then
            Selection.TypeText "    " & docThis.Bookmarks(J).Name
            Selection.TypeParagraph
        End If
    Next J

    Selection.TypeParagraph
    Selection.TypeParagraph
    Selection.TypeText "The following are bookmarks that mark "
    Selection.TypeText "single locations in the document"
    Selection.TypeParagraph

    For J = 1 To docThis.Bookmarks.Count
        If docThis.Bookmarks(J).Empty Then
            Selection.TypeText "    " & docThis.Bookmarks(J).Name
            Selection.TypeParagraph
        End If
    Next J

    Selection.TypeParagraph
    Selection.TypeParagraph
    Selection.TypeText "There are a total of "
    Selection.TypeText docThis.Bookmarks.Count
    Selection.TypeText " bookmarks in the document"
    Selection.TypeParagraph
End Sub
```

The macro creates a new document and puts two lists in it: A list of bookmarks in the original document that refer to text selections and a list of bookmarks that refer to single locations.

Deleting Bookmarks

When your macro no longer needs a bookmark, it can be easily deleted. All you need to do is use the Delete method, in this manner:

```
ActiveDocument.Bookmarks("MyBookmark").Delete
```

This deletes a single bookmark named MyBookmark. If you want to delete all the bookmarks in a document, you can do so in this manner:

```
Dim BkMk As Bookmark

For Each BkMk In ActiveDocument.Bookmarks
    BkMk.Delete
Next BkMk
```

Saving Documents

VBA provides three different methods you can use to save your document: Close, Save, and SaveAs. Each of these is detailed in the following sections.

The Close Method

When you are done processing a document in your macro, chances are good that you'll want to close it. This is done by using the Close method, in this manner:

```
ActiveDocument.Close
```

Of course, you can use a different Document object in place of the ActiveDocument object. The Close method prompts you to save your changes (if necessary) and then closes the document. If you want to close the document without being prompted about saving changes, you can use the following:

```
ActiveDocument.Close(wdDoNotSaveChanges)
```

This results in the changes not being saved; they are discarded. If you would rather simply have any changes saved without being prompted, then you should use the following:

```
ActiveDocument.Close(wdSaveChanges)
```

The Save Method

As you are working with a document, it is good practice to periodically save your changes. This prevents a catastrophe in case your system crashes for some reason. The Save method is the same as clicking the Save icon on the Quick Access Toolbar (it looks like a small diskette).

```
ActiveDocument.Save
```

If the document being saved has not been previously saved, then Word displays the Save As dialog box, described in the next section.

Interestingly, you can use the Save method with the entire Documents collection. This results in all the currently open documents being saved. In this case you would use this command:

```
Documents.Save
```

When you are done using the Save method, the document that was saved is still open in Word. You can do additional processing from that point, or you can close the document as discussed in the previous section.

The SaveAs Method

If you want to save a document using a new name or in a different format, then you'll want to use the SaveAs method if you are using Word 2007 or the SaveAs2 method if you are using Word 2010 or Word 2013. There are a myriad of parameters you can use with either of these methods, but this is typically the bare minimum:

```
ActiveDocument.SaveAs("c:/docplace/mynewdoc.docx")
```

The SaveAs2 method was added in Word 2010, but that doesn't mean that the older SaveAs method won't work. For most purposes, SaveAs works just fine. If you anticipate that your macro may be used on Word 2007 systems, then you'll want to make sure that you don't use SaveAs2; it generates an error.

If you want to set the other parameters available with the SaveAs and SaveAs2 methods, they are as follows and in order:

- **FileName.** The name under which the file should be saved.
- **FileFormat.** A numeric indicator of what file format should be used for the saved file. This indicator seems to change from version to version of Word; check the online help for information on what codes can be used.
- **LockComments.** Set to True if you want the document saved in protected manner, such that only comments can be added to it.
- **Password.** A password subsequently required to open the document.
- **AddToRecentFiles.** Set to True if you want this document added to the MRU list maintained by Word.
- **WritePassword.** A password used in the future if the user wants to save changes.
- **ReadOnlyRecommended.** Set to True if you want the document saved as read-only.
- **EmbedTrueTypeFonts.** Set to True if you want any eligible TrueType fonts saved with the document.
- **SaveNativePictureFormat.** If set to True and the graphics in the document are in non-Windows format, those graphics are converted to and saved only in a native Windows format.
- **SaveFormsData.** Set to True if the document is a form and you only want the form data saved.
- **SaveAsAOCELetter.** Set to True if the document has an attached AOCE letter mailer.
- **Encoding.** The character set to be used when saving the document, particularly if it is being saved in a text format.
- **InsertLineBreaks.** Set to True if you are saving as a text file and you want line breaks inserted at the end of each line of text.

- **AllowSubstitutions.** Set to True if you are saving as a text file and you want to allow Word to substitute some symbols with characters that look similar.

- **LineEnding.** Has meaning for document formats that allow differing paragraph endings, such as text files.

- **AddBiDiMarks.** Set to True if you want Word to add control characters to the file that preserve bi-directional layout of the text. This only has meaning for languages that have right-to-left layout.

- **CompatibilityMode.** An indicator of whether the file should be saved using compatibility mode for use with older versions of Word. (This parameter is only available in the SaveAs2 method.)

Unless you want to actually set each of the parameters under program control, it is usually a good idea to simply use the Save method, instead of the SaveAs method, and allow the user to specify all the parameters in the Save As dialog box.

The SaveAs method is similar in results to the Save method, in that when you are done using it the document that was saved is still open in Word.

11

Working with Selections and Ranges

When working with pieces and parts of a document, the two most common objects you'll work with are either a selection or a range. A *selection* is exactly what it states—the selected portion of a document. You can either start you macro with a selection already made, or you can create a selection within the macro itself.

A *range* is an object in Word. That simple statement belies the power that is contained within ranges. Most objects have, as a child, a Range object that represents the object itself. That may sound a bit odd, but it is the way that the Word object model is built. In many cases where you might expect a property or method to be accessible from an object, it won't be; instead, the property or method is accessible through the child Range object.

As an example, consider the following simple example. You might expect that you could access the text of the fourth paragraph in a document in this manner:

```
sRawText = ActiveDocument.Paragraphs(4).Text
```

This won't work, however. Instead, as you learned in Chapter 10 you need to access the text in this manner:

```
sRawText = ActiveDocument.Paragraphs(4).Range.Text
```

Since both selections and ranges are objects, they are widely and often used in Word macros. Perhaps the biggest difference between them is that there can only be a single Selection object in a given document window, whereas there can be multiple Range objects defined. This means that ranges are much more flexible and important to your programming efforts.

With very few exceptions, you use the exact same techniques to create and work with both selections and ranges. The majority of this chapter uses references that apply to selections, but they could just as easily apply to ranges.

Because of how important both selections and ranges are to your macros, you'll want to pay particular attention to the information in this chapter.

Creating a Selection

When you are creating small macros, a selection is typically whatever was selected by the user before a macro was executed. This is common, as it allows your macro to take its actions using whatever the user selected. There are times, however, when you may want your macro to actually create a selection and then take some action on that selection.

The basic way that you create an extension (and therefore enlarge the selection) is by moving the insertion point. This may sound odd, but remember that the insertion point is always active and always visible within a document. Even if you select a few characters or a paragraph, the insertion point is still there, lurking at the very end of the selection.

You move the insertion point by using one of these basic methods:

- **MoveLeft.** Moves the insertion point to the left.
- **MoveRight.** Moves the insertion point to the right.
- **MoveUp.** Moves the insertion point up.
- **MoveDown.** Moves the insertion point down.

The names of these methods should ring a bell; they have the same effect as pressing the four arrow keys on the keyboard. You can express in the code how many times the movement should occur, like this:

```
Selection.MoveRight Unit:=wdCharacter, Count:=5, Extend:=wdExtend
```

It is the Count variable that tells how many times the movement should occur. In this instance the selection is moved 5 characters to the right. The other two variables indicate what type of units should be used in the move and whether the selection should be extended or not. The default unit that a move uses is wdCharacter, or single characters. You can use any of these units:

- **wdCharacter.** Single characters.
- **wdWord.** Single words.
- **wdSentence.** Single sentences.
- **wdParagraph.** Single paragraphs.
- **wdSection.** Single document sections.
- **wdLine.** Single lines (only works when using MoveUp or MoveDown).
- **wdRow.** Single rows (only works in tables).
- **wdColumn.** Single columns (only works in tables).
- **wdCell.** Single cells (only works in tables).

The Extend variable can have only two settings: wdMove (the default) or wdExtend. If it is set to wdExtend, it is similar to holding down the SHIFT key as you press one of the arrow keys—the result is that the selection is extended as the movement occurs.

As an example, let's say that you want to select the three words to the right of the current insertion point, but you want the word in which the insertion point is located to count as one of those words. This involves the use of two selection movement operations, as follows:

```
Selection.MoveLeft Unit:=wdWord, Count:=1
Selection.MoveRight Unit:=wdWord, Count:=3, Extend:=wdExtend
```

The first line moves the insertion point to the beginning of the word in which the insertion point is located and the second line then extends the selection three words to the right.

Word also provides a number of other selection movement methods: Move, MoveWhile, MoveUntil, MoveStart, MoveStartWhile, MoveStartUntil, MoveEnd, MoveEndWhile, and MoveEndUntil. The use of these methods is beyond the scope of this book, however. You'll find that most of your movement needs can be accommodated with the four basic movement methods already described.

Finding Information about the Selection

When working with the Selection object, Word provides the Information property to return information that you may need about the object. The general way you use this property is as follows:

```
vMyValue = Selection.Information(constant)
```

You need to provide, in place of *constant,* a Word constant that indicates the information you want to access. The Information property can return information of almost any type, which means it can be either numeric or textual. So, unless you know what Word should be returning, it is good to assign the value to a variable using the Variant data type.

The following sections describe the various pieces of information you can get about the selection.

General Information

You can find the following general items concerning the selection:

- **wdCapsLock.** Returns True or False to indicate whether the Caps Lock key is on.
- **wdNumLock.** Returns True or False to indicate whether the Num Lock Key is on.
- **wdOverType.** Returns True or False to indicate whether Word is operating in Overtype mode or not.
- **wdRevisionMarking.** Returns True or False to indicate whether Track Changes is turned on.
- **wdSelectionMode.** Indicate whether the selection is normal (0), a selection in Extend mode (1), or a columnar selection (2).
- **wdZoomPercentage.** The current zoom setting.

As an example, you may create a macro that modifies a document extensively. In such a situation you probably wouldn't want to run the macro if Word's Track Changes feature is enabled. This code determines if Track Changes is turned on and only does its work if it is off.

```
If Not Selection.Information(wdRevisionMarking) Then
    DoProcessing
Else
    MsgBox "Please turn off Track Changes and try again."
End If
```

Note that the DoProcessing procedure is called only if the value returned by the Information property is False. If it is True, then a message box is displayed explaining why the processing isn't taking place.

Selection Information

You may need to know quite a bit of information about the selection itself. The following pieces of information are available, and they all concern either the selection or the location of the insertion point. (In Word, the insertion point is considered a "collapsed" selection, meaning it is a selection that has no length at all.)

- **wdActiveEndAdjustedPageNumber.** The page number on which the selection ends.

- **wdActiveEndPageNumber.** The absolute page number on which the selection ends.

- **wdActiveEndSectionNumber.** The section number in which the selection ends.

- **wdFirstCharacterColumnNumber.** How many characters from the left margin the first character of the selection occurs.

- **wdFirstCharacterLineNumber.** The line number where the first character of the selection occurs on the page where it is located. If operating in Draft, Outline, or Web Layout views, the value returned is -1.

- **wdFrameIsSelected.** Returns True or False to indicate whether the selection includes a frame or text box.

- **wdHeaderFooterType.** Indicates whether the selection is in a header or footer and, if so, which header or footer it is in: not in header or footer (-1), even-page header (0), odd-page header (1), even-page footer (2), odd-page footer (3), first-page header (4), or first-page footer (5).
- **wdHorizontalPositionRelativeToPage.** The number of twips to the selection's left edge from the left edge of the page. (A twip is roughly equivalent to 1/1440 of an inch.)
- **wdHorizontalPositionRelativeToTextBoundary.** The number of twips from the selection's left edge to the left boundary of the text area. (A twip is roughly equivalent to 1/1440 of an inch.)
- **wdInClipboard.** Returns True or False to indicate whether the selection is in the Clipboard pane.
- **wdInCommentPane.** Returns True or False to indicate whether the selection is in the comment pane.
- **wdInEndnote.** Returns True or False to indicate whether the selection is in an endnote.
- **wdInFootnote.** Returns True or False to indicate whether the selection is in a footnote.
- **wdInFootnoteEndnotePane.** Returns True or False to indicate whether the selection is in the notes pane.
- **wdInHeaderFooter.** Returns True or False to indicate if the selection is in a header or footer.
- **wdInMasterDocument.** Returns True or False to indicate if the selection is in a master document that contains at least one subdocument.
- **wdInWordMail.** Indicates whether the selection is part of a WordMail send note (1), part of a WordMail read note (2), or not in WordMail (0).
- **wdNumberOfPagesInDocument.** Returns the number of pages in the document associated with the selection.
- **wdReferenceOfType.** Indicates whether the selection is before a footnote reference (1), before an endnote reference (2), or before a comment reference (3). Returns -1 if the selection includes a reference along with other items or a 0 if the selection is not before a reference.

- **wdVerticalPositionRelativeToPage.** The number of twips to the selection's top edge from the top edge of the page. (A twip is roughly equivalent to 1/1440 of an inch.)
- **wdVerticalPositionRelativeToTextBoundary.** The number of twips from the selection's top edge to the top boundary of the text area. (A twip is roughly equivalent to 1/1440 of an inch.)

If you are creating macros for others to use, you'll end up using quite a few of the Information property settings in this section. For example, it is common to make sure that the insertion point is within the main body of the document before your perform some tasks, such as inserting new text. The way you do this is to check to see if the selection is in some special area of the document, such as a header or a footnote:

```
Dim bOK As Boolean

bNotOK = Selection.Information(wdInHeaderFooter)
bNotOK = bNotOK Or Selection.Information(wdInCommentPane)
bNotOK = bNotOK Or Selection.Information(wdInEndnote)
bNotOK = bNotOK Or Selection.Information(wdInFootnote)
bNotOK = bNotOK Or Selection.Information(wdFrameIsSelected)
bNotOK = bNotOK Or Selection.Information(wdInFootnoteEndnotePane)
bNotOK = bNotOK Or Selection.Information(wdInHeaderFooter)
If bNotOK Then
    MsgBox "Please move to the main document body and try again."
Else
    DoProcessing
End If
```

Table Information

It is also possible that your selection may be within a table or include a table within it. If that is the case, then you'll be interested in the following pieces of information:

- **wdAtEndOfRowMarker.** Returns True or False to indicate whether the selection is at the end-of-row marker.
- **wdEndOfRangeColumnNumber.** The number of the table column in which the selection ends.

- **wdEndOfRangeRowNumber.** The number of the table row in which the selection ends.
- **wdMaximumNumberOfColumns.** The maximum number of columns within the selection.
- **wdMaximumNumberOfRows.** The maximum number of rows within the selection.
- **wdStartOfRangeColumnNumber.** The number of the table column in which the selection starts.
- **wdStartOfRangeRowNumber.** The number of the table row in which the selection starts.
- **wdWithinTable.** Returns True or False to indicate whether the selection is in a table.

Editing the Selection

There are a couple of ways you can perform basic editing functions in Word. One method of doing some basic editing (by working with entire paragraphs) was discussed in Chapter 10. You can also use the Selection object to perform basic editing functions.

Adding Text

Adding text is easy using the Selection object. All you need to do is use the TypeText method, in this manner:

```
Selection.TypeText "Here is the text to add."
```

This simple command line adds the text string to your document at the location of the insertion point. If there is a selection already made when the line is executed, then it normally replaces whatever it is that you had selected. If you don't want to replace what is there, then use one of the following code lines, instead:

```
Selection.InsertBefore "Here is the text to add."
Selection.InsertAfter "Here is the text to add."
```

As you might imagine, these code lines insert text either before or after the current selection. Word also extends the selection to include whatever text you added.

You should note that any of these methods of adding text do just that—they only add the text in the string you specify. They don't insert it as a new paragraph; that is something you do by using the methods in the following section.

Inserting Paragraphs

When you are typing in a document, you indicate the end of a paragraph by pressing the ENTER key. There is no way to press an ENTER key in a macro, but you can simulate one in your typing by using one of the following methods:

- **TypeParagraph.** The exact same as pressing ENTER at the location of the selection.
- **InsertParagraph.** Another way of invoking the TypeParagraph method; does the same thing.
- **InsertParagraphAfter.** Adds an end-of-paragraph mark (presses ENTER) just after the current selection. The selection is extended to include the added paragraph.
- **InsertParagraphBefore.** Adds an end-of-paragraph mark (presses ENTER) just before the current selection. The selection is extended to include the added paragraph.

Here is one way you an insert a paragraph at the current insertion point:

```
Dim sTemp As String

sTemp = "This is a new paragraph that I want added to the document."
Selection.TypeText sTemp
Selection.TypeParagraph
```

Deleting Text

Getting rid of a text selection is easy; all you need to do is use the Delete method:

```
Selection.Delete
```

Whatever is selected when you execute this is deleted. The method has the same effect as pressing the Delete key. That means that if you have nothing selected, then whatever is to the right of the insertion point is deleted when the method is invoked.

Collapsing the Selection

When someone runs a macro, they may have run it with a selection made in the document. You probably noticed that the editing methods described in the previous sections all affect whatever is selected in the document. For instance, if you use the TypeText method to insert text, then it replaces whatever was selected at the time the code is executed.

If you don't want an editing method to affect the selected text, a good way to prevent it is to collapse the selection. There are two ways you can do this:

```
Selection.Collapse Direction:=wdCollapseStart
Selection.Collapse Direction:=wdCollapseEnd
```

These usages of the Collapse method collapse the selection to either the beginning or end of the selection, respectively. This means that the selection is removed (deselected or unselected) and the insertion point is moved to either the beginning or end of what used to previously be the selection.

Creating a Range

A Range object is a portion of a document that you define. Normally this definition occurs automatically when you use a property or method of a Word object that returns a Range. For instance, the following code returns a Range object that represents a paragraph in a document:

```
Dim pr As Range

Set pr = ActiveDocument.Paragraphs(3).Range
```

A Range object can refer to a piece of a document (such as the paragraph in the foregoing example), a single point in a document, or the entire document. This makes Range objects very versatile and they can quickly become the workhorses of your document processing.

It helps to think of a Range as a defined part of a document. When you create a Range object, you specify the part of the document to which it refers. You can then use the Range in other operations, making it easier to reference that element. For example, you might create a Range object that refers to a heading in the document or to a table. How you define and use the Range object is entirely up to you.

Editing a Range

Editing a range is a simple task. All you basically need to do is make sure that your Range object is defined as either a location within your document or a piece of your document. You can then use the Text method to add your text. The following sections demonstrate how this editing technique works.

Adding Text

Inserting text into a document is easy using a Range object. If your range points to a single location within the document, then you simply use the Text method to do the insertion. For instance, the following code inserts text at the end of the document:

```
Dim pr As Range

Set pr = ActiveDocument.Range
pr.Collapse wdCollapseEnd
pr.Text = "This is my new text."
```

The code works because it sets a Range object that is equal to the entire document, then collapses the Range to the end of the document—it is now a single point. The Text method is used to insert the text at that point.

The same technique could be used to add text at the end or beginning of a paragraph, as shown here:

```
Dim pr As Range

Set pr = ActiveDocument.Paragraphs(7).Range
pr.Collapse wdCollapseEnd
pr.Text = "text at end of paragraph"

Set pr = ActiveDocument.Paragraphs(7).Range
pr.Collapse wdCollapseStart
pr.Text = "text at start of paragraph"
```

When you execute this code, what you see may surprise you. The text added at the end of paragraph seven ("text at end of paragraph") actually appears at the beginning of paragraph eight. The reason for this is simple—when you collapse a Range, then the ending point of one paragraph is synonymous with the beginning point of the next paragraph. If you really wanted to add the text to the end of paragraph seven you would need to make an adjustment to the end of the Range before you do the collapse, as shown here:

```
Dim pr As Range

Set pr = ActiveDocument.Paragraphs(7).Range
pr.End = pr.End - 1
pr.Collapse wdCollapseEnd
pr.Text = "[This is the end]"
```

To add a whole new paragraph into a document, all you need to do is make sure that what you are adding contains a vbCrLf combination, in this manner:

```
Dim pr As Range
Dim sMyText As String

sMyText = "This is the full text of my paragraph." & vbCrLf
Set pr = ActiveDocument.Paragraphs(10).Range
pr.Collapse wdCollapseStart
pr.Text = sMyText
```

Replacing Text

Using a Range object and the information you learned in the previous section, you can easily replace existing text. The trick is to make sure that you don't collapse the Range before you use the Text method. For example, if you want to replace the first word in the sixth paragraph of your document with a different word, you could use the following:

```
Dim pr As Range
Dim sNewWord As String

sNewWord = "New "
Set pr = ActiveDocument.Paragraphs(6).Range
Set pr = pr.Words(1)
pr.Text = sNewWord
```

Note that the pr Range object is set twice. The first time it is set equal to the sixth paragraph and the second it is set equal to the first element of the Words collection within that range. The result is that it is then equal to the first word of the sixth paragraph. Also note that the replacement word includes a trailing space. This is because each Word within the Words collection includes any trailing spaces for that word.

Deleting Text

You can delete some text in your document by setting a Range object equal to that text and then using the Delete method. For instance, the following code deletes everything in the fourth paragraph of the document except the first and last letters of the paragraph:

```
Dim pr As Range

Set pr = ActiveDocument.Paragraphs(4).Range
pr.Start = pr.Start + 1
pr.End = pr.End - 2
pr.Delete
```

Note that the Start and End methods are used to modify the beginning and ending points of the Range. The ending point is modified by two characters because the last character of a paragraph is always a carriage return.

12

Working with Tables

The Word object model is very helpful when it comes to working with tables. Each table in your document is a separate object, and all the tables are gathered in the Tables collection. It is more correct to say that a Tables collection consists of all the Table objects in a range, selection, or document. You access the right collection of tables by utilizing the Tables property for a Document, Selection, or Range object.

This chapter helps you understand how to work with tables using VBA. Here you'll discover the following:

- How to create tables from scratch
- Modifying the structure of a table
- Making changes to table properties
- Inserting information within a table
- Getting rid of tables

Creating Tables

You create a new table by using the Add method with the Tables collection. The Add method requires three parameters, as shown here:

```
ActiveDocument.Tables.Add(range, rows, columns)
```

In this example, *range* needs to be a location within the document where you want the table inserted. Normally this is a collapsed Range object that denotes a specific place in the document, but it could be a larger, non-collapsed Range. If it is non-collapsed, then the table being added replaces the text designated by the Range object. The *rows* and *columns* parameters are simple—they specify how many rows and columns you want used in the table.

The following example adds a four-column, five-row table right after the third paragraph in the document:

```
Dim pr As Range
Dim tblNewTable As Table

Set pr = ActiveDocument.Paragraphs(3).Range
pr.Collapse wdCollapseEnd
Set tblNewTable = ActiveDocument.Tables.Add(pr, 5, 4)
```

A table inserted in this way is completely empty and unformatted. This means that it is different than using the Table tool on the Insert tab of the ribbon, as the manual method of adding a table does some minimal formatting (such as adding borders to the table). Later in this chapter you'll discover how to format a table that you've added.

The Add method provides two additional parameters you can optionally use when creating your tables. The first optional parameter is used to specify whether the table columns should automatically resize to fit whatever is placed in the cells. There are two possible settings for this parameter:

- **wdWord8TableBehavior.** Don't resize the columns automatically.
- **wdWord9TableBehavior.** Go ahead and resize the columns automatically, based upon the setting of the next optional parameter.

The second optional parameter only has meaning if the first optional parameter is set to wdWord9TableBehavior. In this case you can specify how you want the resizing done. There are three options:

- **wdAutoFitContent.** Resize the columns to accommodate the content within the column.

- **wdAutoFitWindow.** Resize the columns to accommodate the content in conjunction with the overall space available between the margins.
- **wdAutoFitFixed.** Use fixed column widths.

Changing Table Structure

A Table object contains other collections of objects that are related to the structure of that table. Most notable among the collections are the Rows and Columns collections. Each of these represents the individual rows and columns of the table.

Using these collections you can easily find out the dimensions of a table:

```
Dim iRows As Integer
Dim iCols As Integer
Dim sMessage As String

With ActiveDocument.Tables(1)
    iRows = .Rows.Count
    iCols = .Columns.Count
End With

sMessage = "The table dimensions are " & iRows & " rows "
sMessage = sMessage & "by " & iCols & " columns."
MsgBox sMessage
```

Deleting Rows and Columns

Both the Rows and Columns collections include a Delete method that you can use to get rid of unwanted rows and columns. All you need to do is specify which member of the Rows and Columns collection it is that you want to delete, and VBA takes care of the rest:

```
ActiveDocument.Tables(1).Columns(3).Delete
```

The Delete method actually deletes the row or column from the table, it doesn't just delete the contents of the row or table.

Adding Rows and Columns

Both the Rows and Columns collections allow you to add new rows or columns using the Add method. This method behaves similarly to how the Add method behaves with other collections. Using it is simple:

```
ActiveDocument.Tables(1).Rows.Add
ActiveDocument.Tables(1).Columns.Add
```

These lines add a row to the table after the last row and a column to the table after the last column. If you want to specify where the row or column is added, then things get a bit more complex.

Let's say you want to add a row just before the third row of your table. You can accomplish the task with this code:

```
With ActiveDocument.Tables(1)
    .Rows.Add BeforeRow:=.Rows(3)
End With
```

The optional BeforeRow parameter must be a Row object and specifies the point before which the row is to be added. You can similarly insert a column before a specified column:

```
With ActiveDocument.Tables(1)
    .Columns.Add BeforeColumn:=.Columns(2)
End With
```

A word of caution: Adding columns doesn't resize any of the columns in the table. It is very possible, by adding columns, to extend the table past the right margin of the page. If you add several columns, it is possible to extend the table quite far past the right margin. To make your macro-modified table usable, you'll want to make sure you also adjust column widths when adding columns.

Merging and Splitting Cells

The way in which you merge and split cells in a table, using VBA, is a bit esoteric and counterintuitive. There is a single method used to both merge and split cells: the Split method. If you use the Split method with a single cell, then the format to use is this:

```
ActiveDocument.Tables(1).Cell(2,2).Split rows, columns
```

This example splits the cell at the intersection of row 2 column 2 into however many *rows* and *columns* you specify. Word doesn't require the cell you are splitting to have previously been merged; it splits any cell.

Here's where the counterintuitive part of Split comes into play: If you want to merge together cells in a row, you can still use the Split method to do it. All you need to do is define the group of cells you want to merge, and then provide the parameters for the split:

```
ActiveDocument.Tables(1).Rows(2).Cells.Split 1, 2, True
```

This line takes all the cells in row 2 of the table and then "splits" them into 1 row and 2 columns. In other words, it merges whatever it needs to in order to make sure that the second row consists of only two cells. The True parameter at the end of the command line tells VBA to merge the cells together before it does a split.

A better way to do merges is to use the Merge method. All you need to do is use the Merge method with the upper-left cell in the group of cells you want to merge and then provide the reference to the cell at the lower-right corner of the group:

```
With ActiveDocument.Tables(1)
    .Cell(2, 2).Merge .Cell(4, 3)
End With
```

This code merges the cells in the block defined by the cell at row 2, column 2 and row 4, column 3. Figure 12-1 shows what the table looks like both before and after the merge.

Changing Table Characteristics

Each table you create has certain characteristics relating to size and appearance. You may want to change these characteristics in your macro, and Word provides plenty of ways to do that. Three of the most common characteristics you might want to change are row height, column width, and the font specs used for table content.

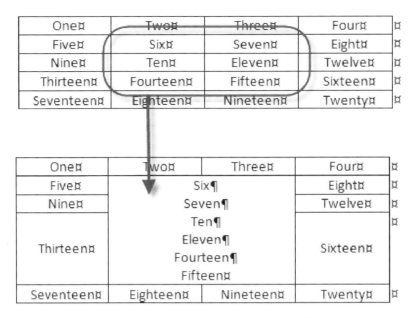

Figure 12-1. A table before and after a cell merge.

Changing Row Height and Column Width

Each row of a table has an associated Height property and each column has a Width property. You can modify these properties as desired. For instance, the following changes the width of the second column in a table:

```
ActiveDocument.Tables(1).Columns(2).Width = 100
```

Similarly, the following changes the height of a row in the same table:

```
ActiveDocument.Tables(1).Rows(5).Height = 19
```

Both the Height and Width properties are specified in points.

Changing Formatting

If you want to modify the format of a particular cell, row, or column, the easiest way to do so is to use the Font object that belongs to whatever you want to change. For instance, let's say that you want to make the third row of a table bold and dark blue. You can do so by using this code:

```
With ActiveDocument.Tables(1).Rows(3).Range.Font
    .Color = wdColorDarkBlue
    .Bold = True
End With
```

You can pick other elements of a table to change by simply changing the Rows reference to whatever it is you want to change.

Adding Information to Tables

There are a variety of ways that you can add content to the cells in a table. The methods differ in how you specify which cell should receive your content. The first method requires that you use the Cells collection to specify a row and column for the content. This code, for example, specifies you want to add information to the second row, fourth cell:

```
ActiveDocument.Tables(1).Cell(2, 4)
```

You can also specify a location by position within a row:

```
ActiveDocument.Tables(1).Rows(2).Cells(4)
```

The third method of addressing where information goes is similar, but focuses on the column in which the information should go:

```
ActiveDocument.Tables(1).Columns(4).Cells(2)
```

The second and third methods of addressing cells are only available if there are no merged cells in the row or column being addressed. If there are, then you must use the first method.

Let's create a simple example of how to add information to a table. We'll create a macro that adds a table and then steps through each cell in the table, stuffing a word in that cell. The problem, of course, is what to stuff in the table. We'll get around this problem by grabbing the first group of words from the document and stuffing those into the table. This macro checks to make sure there are no existing tables in the document; if there are, it won't run.

```
Sub FillTable()
    Dim iRow As Integer
    Dim iCol As Integer
```

```
        Dim J As Integer
        Dim sWord As String
        Dim pr As Range
        Dim tbl As Table

        If ActiveDocument.Tables.Count = 0 Then
            Set pr = ActiveDocument.Range
            pr.Collapse wdCollapseEnd
            Set tbl = ActiveDocument.Tables.Add(pr, 5, 4)
            J = 0
            For iRow = 1 To 5
                For iCol = 1 To 4
                    sWord = ""
                    While (Len(sWord) = 0) Or (sWord = vbCr)
                        J = J + 1
                        sWord = Trim(ActiveDocument.Words(J))
                    Wend
                    tbl.Cell(iRow, iCol).Range.Text = sWord
                Next iCol
            Next iRow
        End If
End Sub
```

Once the macro determines there are no tables in the document, it adds a new table at the end. Then it starts stepping through each cell of the table. For each cell it grabs the next real word from the document and stuffs that word into the cell.

Deleting Tables

The easiest way to delete a table is to simply use the Delete method with the Tables collection. For instance, you could delete the first table in a document in this manner:

```
ActiveDocument.Tables(1).Delete
```

If you have a number of tables in your document, you'll want to make sure that you delete the one you really want to delete. If you decide you want to delete all the tables in the document you can do so by using a For Each loop:

```
Dim tbl As Table

For Each tbl in ActiveDocument.Tables
    tbl.Delete
Next tbl
```

13

Searching and Replacing

One of the most powerful editing tools that Word provides is the Find and Replace tool. This tool can be just as powerful when you are using it under the control of your macros. The only thing you need to master when it comes to finding things is the Find object. Secondary to the Find object is the Replacement object, which allows you to replace whatever you are able to find.

This chapter focuses on the ways you can use Find and Replace within your macro code. When you are done you'll be able to whip through a find and replace in no time.

Finding Things

At the root of using Find and Replace within your macro is the Find object. The easiest way to see how Word puts this object together is to record a macro that looks for something simple. For instance, let's say you want to search for instances of the word *Note*. Perform these steps if you are using Word 2007:

1. Display the Developer tab of the ribbon.
2. Click the Record Macro tool. Word displays the Record Macro dialog box, as shown in Figure 13-1.
3. Click OK. Word starts the recording process.
4. Display the Find tab of the Find and Replace dialog box, shown in Figure 13-2. (In Word 2007 press CTRL+F. In Word 2010 and Word 2013

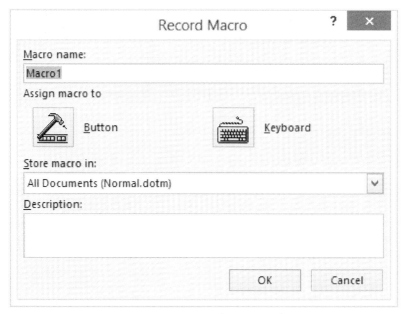

Figure 13-1. Getting ready to record a macro.

Figure 13-2. Searching for something in Word.

display the Home tab of the ribbon, click the down-arrow next to the Find tool, then choose Advanced Find.)

5. In the Find What box, enter the word **Note**.
6. Click Find Next.

7. Press **Esc** to dismiss the Find and Replace dialog box.
8. On the Developer tab of the ribbon click the Stop Recording tool.

The macro recorder dutifully records your actions and you end up with a macro that looks very similar to this:

```
Sub Macro1()
'
' Macro1 Macro
'
'
    Selection.Find.ClearFormatting
    With Selection.Find
        .Text = "Note"
        .Replacement.Text = ""
        .Forward = True
        .Wrap = wdFindContinue
        .Format = False
        .MatchCase = False
        .MatchWholeWord = False
        .MatchWildcards = False
        .MatchSoundsLike = False
        .MatchAllWordForms = False
    End With
    Selection.Find.Execute
End Sub
```

Note the use of the Find object, which makes up the bulk of this macro. There are three uses of the object; the first uses the ClearFormatting method, the second sets quite a few properties for the object, and the third uses the Execute method. These invocations are instructive in how to use the Find object, but they don't show you some of the real power behind what you can do with it.

Find Properties

The bulk of the recorded macro shown in the previous section dealt with setting properties. These properties define exactly how the Find object is to actually do its searching. Here are the properties you are most likely to use; you'll notice several from this list were used by Word in the recorded macro.

- **Font.** Specifies the character formatting to be matched in the search. This is actually a Font object, so many elements can be specified when it comes to formatting.

- **Format.** True or False, indicating if formatting is to be considered when searching.
- **Forward.** True or False, indicating the direction of the search (True goes forward, False goes backward).
- **Highlight.** True or False, indicating if the text being searched for is highlighted.
- **IgnorePunct.** True or False, indicating whether punctuation should be ignored when searching.
- **IgnoreSpace.** True or False, indicating whether white space should be ignored when searching.
- **MatchAllWordForms.** True or False, indicating whether all forms of a word should be considered a match when searching.
- **MatchCase.** True or False, indicating if the search should be sensitive to letter case.
- **MatchPhrase.** True or False, indicating if the search should ignore white space and control characters between words.
- **MatchSoundsLike.** True or False, indicating if words that sound similar to the search word should be considered a match.
- **MatchWholeWord.** True or False, indicating if the search should only find complete words that match the search word.
- **MatchWildcards.** True or False, indicating whether Word should use pattern matching.
- **NoProofing.** True or False, indicating whether Word should consider or ignore text that the spelling and grammar tools ignore.
- **ParagraphFormat.** Specifies the paragraph formatting to be matched in the search. This is actually a ParagraphFormat object, so many elements can be specified when it comes to paragraph formatting.
- **Style.** Specifies the style for the search.
- **Text.** The text to be found.
- **Wrap.** Specifies what should happen if the search begins at a place other than the beginning of the document and the end or beginning (depending on direction) of the document is reached.

You should understand that the properties are somewhat persistent in nature. In other words, if you do a search and set some of the properties (either manually or using a macro), then the next time you do a search those properties are still set. Thus, it is a good idea to make sure you always completely set whatever properties you need for your search.

Executing a Search

Once you set the appropriate properties of the Find object, you are ready to begin your search. You do this by using the Execute method:

```
Selection.Find.Execute
```

Once executed, a search sets the Found property of the Find object to indicate the status of the search. If something was found by the search then the Found property is True. This allows you to rapidly perform multiple searches, as shown here:

```
Dim iMyCount As Integer

iMyCount = 0
With Selection.Find
    .ClearFormatting
    .Text = "Note"
    .Forward = True
    .Wrap = wdFindContinue
    .Format = False
    .MatchCase = False
    .MatchWholeWord = False
    .MatchWildcards = False
    .MatchSoundsLike = False
    .MatchAllWordForms = False
    .Execute
    While .Found
        iMyCount = iMyCount + 1
        .Execute
    Wend
End With

MsgBox "There were " & iMyCount & " instances of 'Note'"
```

This code sets up the Find object, executes it once to initially set the Found property, and then loops through multiple executions until the text is no longer located. (In other words, as long as the Found property remains True, then another Execute method is performed.) Each time through the loop the iMyCount variable is incremented, and when the code is complete then the findings are shown in a message box.

Using Find to Modify Your Document

You know that you can use Find and Replace to modify the contents of your document. How you do that is detailed a bit later in this chapter. However, your macro can greatly modify what is in your document in ways that a simple Find and Replace could never do.

The idea is to search for something and then, each time it is found, add or delete text from the document as necessary. As an example, let's say that you receive a document from a co-worker and he formatted all the headings using the Heading 2 style. This isn't a big problem, but you notice that all the text in those headings is lowercase. You'd rather have the headings all be "title case," meaning that only the initial letter of each word is capitalized.

Getting this task accomplished using Find and Replace is nearly impossible, and doing the changes manually could take a long time. This is where a small macro could save you hours of work. All you need to do is use the Find object to look for all the paragraphs formatted with the Heading 2 style. Each time a heading is located, you could then make sure that the correct capitalization is applied.

```
Sub ChangeHeadingCase()
    With Selection.Find
        .ClearFormatting
        .Wrap = wdFindContinue
        .Forward = True
        .Format = True
        .MatchWildcards = False
        .Text = ""
        .Style = ActiveDocument.Styles("Heading 2")
        .Execute
        While .Found
            Selection.Range.Case = wdTitleWord
            Selection.Collapse Direction:=wdCollapseEnd
            .Execute
        Wend
    End With
End Sub
```

Even in a very long document with lots of headings, this macro takes only a couple of seconds to run. The time savings can be immeasurable.

Another example of how you can use the Find object to modify your documents is if you want to make sure that every time your document includes a colon, a space, and a lowercase letter, you want to convert the letter to uppercase. The following macro handles this type of requirement very nicely:

```
Sub CapsAfterColon()
    With Selection.Find
        .ClearFormatting
        .Text = ": ([a-z])"
        .Forward = True
        .Wrap = wdFindContinue
        .Format = True
        .MatchCase = False
        .MatchWholeWord = False
        .MatchWildcards = True
        .MatchSoundsLike = False
        .MatchAllWordForms = False
        .Execute
        While .Found
            Selection.Range.Case = wdUpperCase
            Selection.Collapse Direction:=wdCollapseEnd
            .Execute
        Wend
    End With
End Sub
```

This example of the Find object uses a wildcard search, which makes finding the lowercase letter quite efficient.

Replacing Things

When it comes time to replace things that you've found (using the Find object), Word provides the Replacement object. This object is actually a member of the Find object. For instance, let's say that you wanted to replace all instances of the word *Note* with the word *Important*. You could do that by simply building on how you searched earlier in this chapter:

```
    iMyCount = 0
    With Selection.Find
        .ClearFormatting
        .Text = "Note"
        .Forward = True
        .Wrap = wdFindContinue
        .Format = False
        .MatchCase = False
        .MatchWholeWord = False
        .MatchWildcards = False
        .MatchSoundsLike = False
        .MatchAllWordForms = False
        With .Replacement
            .ClearFormatting
            .Text = "Important"
        Wend
        .Execute Replace:=wdReplaceAll
    End With
```

Note that the Replacement object has its own properties that you can set. These properties are essentially a subset of the properties for the Find object:

- **Font.** Specifies the character formatting to be used in the replacement. This is actually a Font object, so many elements can be specified when it comes to formatting.
- **Highlight.** True or False, indicating if the replacement text should be highlighted.
- **NoProofing.** True or False, indicating whether Word should consider or ignore text that the spelling and grammar tools ignore.
- **ParagraphFormat.** Specifies the paragraph formatting to be used in the replacement. This is actually a ParagraphFormat object, so many elements can be specified when it comes to paragraph formatting.
- **Style.** Specifies the style for any matches made.
- **Text.** The text to be used as the replacement.

Besides setting the properties of the Replacement object, note that the Execute method (which still belongs to the Find object) is invoked with a difference: a setting for the Replace parameter. There are actually three possible settings for this parameter, as follows:

- **wdReplaceNone.** This parameter is the default; it is equivalent to doing a find only, without any replacements being made. It results in the settings in the Replacement object being ignored.
- **wdReplaceAll.** Replace only the next match found.
- **wdReplaceOne.** Replace all matches found in the document.

14

Working with Non-Document Files

All the VBA programs you have created thus far have accessed information typed in by an end user or existing within a Word document. Although this may be sufficient for some macros, it is inevitable that you'll need to read data from or write data to a disk file.

Unless you use data files, your programs will never be able to remember what the user of the program did the last time they ran the program. Data files are used to store information so it can be retrieved at some time in the future when you again run your VBA program.

Sometimes files are used to store configuration information such as the user's name and their preferred options. Other times, files are used to remember aspects such as the last invoice number used or the last date a macro was used. Other times, data files are used to store database information such as data about customers and orders. All these reasons and many more are valid reasons to create and use your own data files in a VBA macro.

In this chapter, you'll uncover the types of data files that you may need to access from within a macro and cover how to do so using VBA.

File Types

Files are used for a wide variety of purposes on computers. Almost every commercial program, including Word, uses files in one way or another. These programs create and maintain files with information for their own use or to share with other programs.

There are numerous types of files that you can have on your computer. Typically the file's extension (the portion of the filename after the period) identifies what type of file it is, although nothing forces this identification except tradition.

Although each file extension typically identifies the file type, most file types are only understood by the programs that uses them. Windows does not know one type of file from the next—at least not from the filename alone. Typically, Windows only sees a file as being a series of characters that can be interpreted in any number of ways. The format of a file is usually determined by the program that uses it.

Although Windows does not typically care about specific types of files, there are different formats that can be used by and are used by various programs. You need to read and update each of these formats differently. The remainder of this section discusses these different kinds of formats:

- Text files
- Foreign file formats
- Import/Export formats
- Initialization (.INI) files
- Simple multiple record databases.

Text Files

ASCII stands for American Standard Code for Information Interchange and it defines standard characters for interchanging information on a computer. In ASCII, each character is assigned a numeric code that is used to represent and store that character in a file. The printable characters defined by ASCII are 32 (a space) through 126 (a tilde: "~").

A true ASCII text file is one that contains a series of printable characters separated by a carriage return (ASCII value of 13) and a line feed character

(ASCII value of 10). Each of these carriage return/line feed pairs denotes the end of a line and the beginning of another line.

ASCII text files are probably the most common file format used by your PC. Virtually every program that can read and write files can read and write ASCII text files. The Notepad accessory, provided with Windows, can read and write ASCII text files just fine.

In addition, VBA provides statements and functions that make reading and writing ASCII text files line by line a breeze. Those statements are covered in detail later in this chapter.

Foreign File Formats

Many programs maintain information in their own special file formats. These formats are simply layouts that were created for use with the program because the program's developers decided it was best for them to store their data in that manner.

There are many examples of different types of data formats. For example, Word stores its documents in .DOCX and .DOCM files and its templates in .DOTX and DOTM files. Other programs—like Excel, Access, and PowerPoint—store their files using different formats. The list could go on and on.

These file formats were originally designed by the developer(s) of the program. Some of these formats have been published so that anyone who wants to read and update them can do so. Other formats are considered trade secrets and the only way to figure them out (short of hiring a spy) is to spend a lot of time with a program that lets you look at each character in the file—although this is much like trying to learn French by picking up a book written in French and simply trying to read it. Some people can do it, but it takes a long time and a lot of perseverance!

Provided you know the format of a specific file, you can write routines in VBA to read, write, and update any foreign file type you want. This writing is done using the binary file processing capability of the language, which is covered later in this chapter.

Import/Export Formats

Although many programs maintain information in files of their own format, there are several common file interchange formats used for importing and exporting into and out of programs. These common formats are understood by many programs and facilitate the transfer of information from one program to the next.

Examples of these format types are the Rich Text Format (.RTF) for transferring word processing files from one word processor to the next. Another example is an older format known as the Data Interchange Format (.DIF) which is used to transfer information from one spreadsheet program to another. There are many other special formats in use today, and there will be many more designed and used in the future.

Often these import/export file formats are simply specially formatted ASCII text files. These types of files can be easily viewed and edited with a text editor such as Notepad. Even so, these files contain additional information needed by programs during the import of the data.

VBA provides direct support for an import/export format often referred to as a *delimited text file*. Here's an example of what the contents of such a file might look like:

```
"Mike Schinkel",31,"Atlanta","GA"
"Michelle Brookshire",26,"Clermont","GA"
"Matt Adams",30,"Buford","GA"
"Traci Detchon",36,"Smyrna","GA"
```

Using either VBA's ASCII or binary file processing capability, you have the tools you need to process any type of import/export file that you may find.

File Basics

Because data files are external to your programs, you must take certain steps to allow your program to access the information contained in the files. Essentially, your macro must establish a line of communication with a file before it can process it. When you finish using a file, you should cut off that line of communication because each open line of communication requires resources to maintain.

Opening a File

In the same way you open the door of a filing cabinet before you can browse through its files, your VBA code must open a file before it can read or update its contents. The statement to do this is Open. Using only its most basic options, you can open files for reading (Input), writing (Output), or appending (Append).

The basic format for the Open statement is

```
Open filename [for mode] As filenum
```

You must use Open before attempting to read or write from the file. The *filename* parameter must be a valid filename. The optional *mode* specifier can be any of these: Input, Output, or Append. Finally, the *filenum* can be any integer value from 1 to 255. Here are some examples:

```
Open "c:\someplace\myfile.txt" For Input As 1
Open "errorlog.txt" For Append As 2
```

When you open a file you must specify a file number. This file number is subsequently used to refer to the line of communication between your macro and the file on disk. Whenever you need to read from, write to, or otherwise manipulate an open file, you need to use the file number you specified when you opened the file.

The mode that you specify when you open the file is important as well. If you open a file for Input, then you will only be able to read from the file. If you open it for Output, you will only be able to write to the file and VBA starts writing to the file at the beginning. (This presents the very real possibility of wiping out and overwriting an existing file.) If you instead specify Append, you can only write to the file, but VBA starts writing at the end if the file already exists. You learn how to both read and write to the same open file later in this chapter.

Handling File Errors

When you open a file, there is unfortunately a good chance that something could go wrong—for example, the file could be missing. Because of this fact, you must be sure to provide error handling for any routines that open files.

The easiest way for you to handle an error on the Open statement is to use On Error Resume Next and then check the Err function afterwards. The Err function returns a non-zero number identifying the error if an error did occur on the Open statement. The values returned by the Err function are listed in VBA's online help system.

The following example illustrates how to trap and identify file errors; you yourself have to determine what to do in case of an error, as the error handling required for each is likely to be different.

```
On Error Resume Next
Open "c:\myfile.txt" For Input As 3
If Err <> 0 Then
    MsgBox ("File Error: " + Str$(Err))
End If
```

Reading Data Files

After opening a file, the easiest way to read from it is to read the entire file. You can do this using a combination of the two functions: Input and Lof. The Input function reads data from a file and returns it as a string.

You should use the Input function with a file opened using the Input mode of the Open statement. You specify two parameters with the function: the number of bytes (characters) to read from the file and the file number you specified when you opened the file. Here's a simple example that reads 1,024 bytes from a file:

```
Dim sRawText As String

Open "c:\myfile.sys" For Input As 3
sRawText = Input(1024, 3)
```

The Lof function is used to figure out the length of a file. It returns the number of bytes in a file. For instance, this is how you would determine the length of a specific file on your system:

```
Dim lFileSize As Long

Open "c:\someplace\mybigfile.txt" For Input As 1
lFileSize = Lof(1)
```

You can use the Input function with the Lof function to retrieve an entire file into a string variable. This technique is one of the simplest ways of reading a file, but you won't want to read very large files in this manner. Here's the technique for reading the file:

```
Dim sFileText As String

Open "c:\myfile.txt" For Input As 5
sFileText= Input(Lof(5), 5)
```

Closing Files

Just as it is a good idea to close your file cabinet drawers after you are through with them (so you don't bang your shin!), you should also close your program's data files as soon as you no longer need to have them open. A simple Close statement is all that is required to release the line of communication between the program and the file.

You can use Close with or without a file number. If you use a file number, it should be the number of a file you previously opened. If you don't use a file number, then the statement closes any files you previously opened. Either of these is an acceptable use of Close:

```
Close
Close 2
```

It is a good idea for you to close a file as soon as possible to avoid potential problems. Because Windows does not always write information to the disk when you expect it to (it waits until an internal output buffer is full), you cannot be sure that what you sent to the file is actually written to it until you close the file. Because it is better to be safe than sorry, close the file as soon as you can.

Types of File Access

There are three file access modes you can use when working with files:

- Sequential access
- Random access
- Binary access

As discussed earlier, each of these three methods of accessing files has its own particular purpose.

Sequential Files

A sequential file is one written and read from the beginning to the end, in order, much like how tape is played in a tape player. The typical tape player cannot skip to the next song on the tape; instead, it must play or fast-forward through the entire song.

So, a sequential file is one that you can only read in the order that it was written. The reason for this is there is no predetermined structure, and there are no clues for what data is located where.

Reading ASCII Text Files

A perfect example of a sequential file is an ASCII text file. A text editor such as Notepad reads an ASCII text file line by line into memory and then later writes the entire file back out to disk, typically overwriting the previous copy of the file.

In your VBA programs, you may want to read ASCII text files so you can modify them. For example, you may want to update your AUTOEXEC.BAT PATH statement. Or, you may want to write a utility to extract information like the names of subroutines and functions from the VBA code you may export to a disk file (see Chapter 5). Or, you can choose from a multitude of other tasks you can accomplish.

To read the data in an ASCII text file, you must first open the file for input and then you can use the Line Input # statement. Here is how you use the statement:

```
Dim sRawText As String

Open "myfile.txt" For Input As 3
Line Input #3, sRawText
```

You should note that the # mark is necessary in this statement. Without it, VBA generates an error. The Line Input # statement reads a line from the specified file into the string variable you supply.

As mentioned earlier, you can use the Line Input # statement to read a line in an ASCII text file, but ASCII text files often contain more than one line. Obviously, you may need to read more than one line so what do you do? Do you use two Line Input # statements to read two lines, three statements to read three lines, and so on? Of course not! You read lines inside a loop such as a While loop.

But that creates another problem—how do you know when you've reached the last line in the file? Easy. VBA provides an Eof (end-of-file) function that tells you when you have read the last line in the file (but not before).

As an example, assume that you have a file on your system that consists of individual lines of data. Some of the lines of data begin with the characters "CTL" and others begin with the characters "DET". You may want to pull all the lines beginning with "DET" and display them. Here's how you do it:

```
Sub DisplayDetail()
    Dim sTemp As String
    Dim sMessage As String

    On Error Resume Next
    Open "myfile.txt" For Input As 3
    If Err = 0 Then
        sMessage = ""
        Do Until Eof(3)
            Line Input #3, sTemp
            If Left(sTemp, 3) = "DET" Then
                sMessage = sMessage & Mid(sTemp, 4) & vbCrLf
            End If
```

```
        Loop
        Close 3
    Else
        sMessage = "Error opening file"
    End If
    MsgBox sMessage
End Sub
```

Writing to ASCII Text Files

Now that you have read ASCII text files in, you may want to learn how to write them out as well. You write ASCII text files out by using the Print # statement. There are two forms of the Print # statement, as shown here:

```
Print #2, "My text"
Print #2, "My text";
```

Note that the only difference between the two is the semicolon at the end. The difference is that without the semicolon, VBA considers the line "complete" and terminates it with a carriage return/line feed pair. If you don't want the line to be terminated, then include the semicolon.

Suppose you want to update the macro introduced in the previous section so that the detail information is extracted from one file and written out to another file.

```
Sub ExtractDetail()
    Dim sTemp As String
    Dim sMessage As String
    Dim iLines As Integer

    iLines = 0
    On Error Resume Next
    Open "myfile.txt" For Input As 3
    If Err = 0 Then
        Open "extractfile.txt" For Output As 4
        If Err = 0 Then
            sMessage = ""
            Do Until Eof(3)
                Line Input #3, sTemp
                If Left(sTemp, 3) = "DET" Then
                    Print #4, Mid(sTemp, 4)
                    iLines = iLines + 1
                End If
```

```
            Loop
            sMessage = iLines & " lines transferred"
        Else
            sMessage = "Error opening output file"
        End If
    Else
        sMessage = "Error opening input file"
    End If
    Close
    MsgBox sMessage
End Sub
```

Reading Delimited Text Files

As stated earlier, a delimited text file is an ASCII file, but it is an ASCII file for which VBA provides some special processing capabilities. Often you may use these file formats to import from or export to database or spreadsheets programs.

To read delimited text files, you can use the Input # statement. The basic format for the statement is:

```
Input #filenum, var1 [, var2] [..., varN]
```

The Input # statement reads a line from the file identified by *filenum* and parses the information in the file into the variables *var1* through *varN* that you specify. For example:

```
Dim sFullName As String
Dim iAge As Integer
Dim sCity As String
Dim sState As String

Open "myfile.csv" For Input As 1
Input #1, sFullName, iAge, sCity, sState
```

When you use the Input # statement, you must be sure that the file you are reading and the variables you are using coincide in number and in type. If you do not specify enough variables to hold all the data to be read in or if you specify too few, VBA gets confused and you end up getting garbage in your variables.

Writing Delimited Text Files

The converse of the Input # statement is the Write # statement. This statement creates a file that can be read back into numerous other programs or into VBA using the Input # statement:

```
Dim sFullName As String
Dim iAge As Integer
Dim sCity As String
Dim sState As String

Open "myfile.csv" For Ouput As 3
Write #3, sFullName, iAge, sCity, sState
```

Random-Access Files

As compared to a sequential file, a random-access file is one that can be read and written in any order. You may want to think of a random-access file as being like a CD instead of a cassette tape. Just like a compact disc where you can select and play tracks in any order, you can read, write, and even update portions of a random-access file in any order.

Random-access files were originally provided to allow BASIC programmers an easy way to create databases. What is a database? A database is simply a collection of related information organized in a structured way. In earlier days, BASIC programmers created relatively sophisticated database applications using random-access files as the tables in a relational database. Today, however, you would probably not want to use random-access files to implement a complex database program. VBA provides much greater database capabilities via the powerful Access Database Engine. (How you do this is beyond the scope of this book.)

Random-access files are useful if you need to create a relatively simple database or if you need to read and update data that was created by a program that uses that format.

Record Variables: User-Defined Types

Processing random-access files means processing records. As such, you must define the records in your file, which is done by creating a user-defined data type, as first discussed in Chapter 8. Using the Type…End Type data structure you can define how the records in your file should look. Then you can create variables using your definition and store the values contained in these variables directly into the records of your random-access file.

This format for the Type…End Type statement is illustrated in this example:

```
Type GolfCart
    Model As String * 10
    Color As String * 15
    Seats As Integer
    Horses As Single
End Type
```

Use the Type…End Type statement to define the structure of a record in your random-access file. In this example a new data type called GolfCart is created. It consists of four different "member" variables. The first two are strings; Model is 10 characters long and Color is 15. These are followed by Seats (an integer value) and Horses (a single-precision floating-point value).

The new data type must be added to the Declarations area of your modules. You do that by simply using the Procedure drop-down list in the upper-right corner of the Code window to specify the (Declarations) area, as shown in Figure 14-1.

Once defined, you can then use the new user-defined data type in your macro:

```
Dim MyCart As GolfCart
MyCart.Model = "Bogie XL"
MyCart.Color = "Fairway Green"
MyCart.Seats = 2
MyCart.Horses = 10
```

In this example a variable called MyCart is declared as using the GolfCart data type. Values are assigned to individual members of the MyCart variable by separating the variable name (MyCart) from the member names (Model, Color, Seats, and Horses) with a period. This method of addressing members is consistent with how VBA addresses other objects and members.

You must be aware of the size of the structure (in bytes) that you create using the Type…End Type statement. This awareness is important when you open the random-access file, as discussed in the next section. The easiest way to

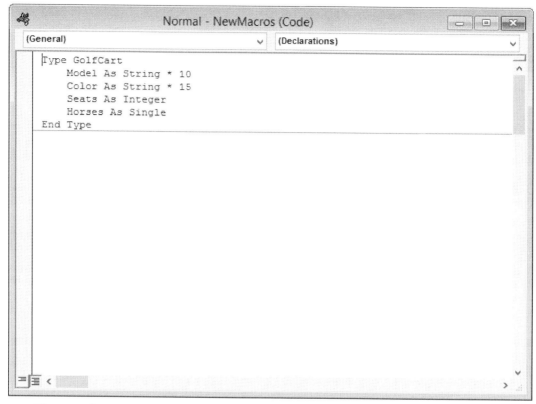

Figure 14-1. Your user-defined data types must be added in the (Declarations) area.

determine the length of your records is by using the Len function. For example you could determine the length of the MyCart variable using a single line of code:

```
iRecLen = Len(MyCart)
```

Opening Random-Access Files

To open a file for random-access, you should specify For Random in the Open statement instead of Input, Output, or Append. In addition, you should specify the record size in bytes using the Len= clause:

```
Open "myfile.dat" For Random As 3 Len = iRecLen
```

Reading Records from Random-access Files

When you have a file open for random access, you can read any record simply by using the Get statement. This statement reads a specific record number into the variable you indicate. For instance, the following example fetches the fifth record from the file and places its contents in the MyCart variable:

```
Get #3, 5, MyCart
```

You can omit the record number in the Get statement if you want. If you use Get without a record number then it fetches the next record from the file:

```
Get #3, , MyCart
```

Listing 10.9 provides a simple example of reading records from a file sequentially using the Get statement.

```
Dim MyCart As GolfCart
Dim iRecLen As Integer
Dim lRecNum As Long
Dim J As Integer

iRecLen = Len(MyCart)
Open "myfile.dat" For Random As 3 Len = iRecLen
lRecNum = Lof(3) / iRecLen

Dim Carts(lRecNum) As GolfCart

For J = 1 to lRecNum
    Get #3, , Carts(J)
Next J
Close 3
```

Although you have seen how to read records sequentially using the Get statement, you can read them in any order. You only need be careful that you do not read a record that does not yet exist in the file; if you attempt to do so, VBA triggers an error.

Writing Records to Random-Access Files

The converse of the Get statement is the Put statement. It is used to write records to a random-access file. All you need to do is make sure you supply a record number and a variable that you want written:

```
Put #3, 5, MyCart
```

If you leave off the record number then Put writes the next record in the file:

```
Put #3, , MyCart
```

To be clear, leaving off the record number causes Put to write to the next record in the file, not to necessarily add a record to the file. Where the next record is located depends on where the previous Get read from or where the previous Put wrote to. Because of this, you'll want to be careful that you don't overwrite any previously saved file information.

Binary Files

As compared to both sequential and random-access files which access files essentially at the record level, binary files are accessed byte by byte. As such, binary files have no limitations whatsoever; you can process a binary file any way you like (assuming that you designed the format of the file). On the other hand, nothing is done for you automatically with binary files; you must determine exactly where to place data into the file and then specify that information to VBA.

Actually, there is no such thing as a binary file; any file can be opened for binary access. You can read, write, and update information for every type of file ever created on a PC using binary mode, assuming that you know the file's format!

Opening Files for Binary Access

To open a file for binary access, you should specify For Binary on the Open statement. Because binary files are accessed byte by byte, you do not need to specify a Len clause as you did for random-access files:

```
Open "c:\someplace\MyCustomers.dat" For Binary As 5
```

Reading from Binary Access Files

When you have opened a file for binary access, you can use the Get statement to read information from the file into variables. You can also specify where in the file you want reading to start:

    Get #5, 100, sTemp

In this case the Get statement reads the file starting with byte 100 and places the input into the sTemp string. You could also read from the current file location by leaving out the start specification:

    Get #5, , sTemp

You need to make sure that sTemp is the length you want before you try to use Get; it is the length of the variable that determines how many bytes are read from the file. In other words, if you want to make sure that 25 bytes are read from the file, you just need to set the length of the variable before using Get:

    sTemp = Space(25)
    Get #5, 100, sTemp

Writing to Binary-Access Files

Writing to a binary file is as easy as reading; you simply use the Put statement to write information from a variable into the file:

    Put #5, 100, sTemp

The Put statement writes the contents of sTemp to the file, starting at (in this case) byte 100. The length of sTemp determines how many bytes are written to the file. The starting position is optional and, if omitted, the Put statement writes to the file starting at the next byte in the file.

Updating the Current Position in a Binary File

If you use binary-access files you may need to move to a specific position in a file so you can begin accessing a portion of the file in a sequential manner. You can use the Seek statement to update the current file position. All you need to do is provide the file number and the position within the file:

```
Seek #3, 200
```

The Seek statement updates the current file pointer position for the file so that the next byte, read or written, is the byte you specified.

Determining the Current Position in a Binary File

As you start to work with binary files, you soon find out that there are two positions that are of importance: the last byte processed and the next byte to be processed. These positions are always offset from each other by one byte.

The last byte processed is determined with the Loc statement, in this manner:

```
Dim lFilePostion As Long
Dim lNextWrite As Long

lFilePosition = Loc(3)
```

If you had just written 150 bytes to the beginning of file 3, then after the above code lFilePosition would be equal to 150. You can find out where the next data will be written by using the Seek statement without a position specification, in this manner:

```
lNextWrite = Seek(3)
```

In this case lNextWrite would be equal to 151, which is where the next writing will occur.

You can use Seek (or Loc) to save and later restore your positions in a binary file as shown here:

```
Dim iSavePos As Integer

Open "orders.dbf" For Binary As #3
iSavePos = Seek(3)      'Get current position
...                     'Do something here
Seek #3, iSavePos       'Return to previous position
```

15

Debugging and Error Handling

Debugging is the process of removing bugs from a program. You wouldn't have to debug your programs if you just didn't put bugs into them in the first place. Unfortunately, programming is a process which is prone to errors. It is sometimes difficult for you to express your ideas with words and, after all, words are a significant part of what you use to program computers.

In this chapter you learn how you can use the tools provided with VBA to debug your programs. You'll also learn some techniques that you can apply during the development process—techniques that can greatly diminish the potential for bugs creeping in your programs in the first place.

What Are Bugs?

If you look in a good programmer's dictionary, you discover that bugs are errors either in hardware or software that cause a computer operation to malfunction. That is not all, however. Bugs also can cause hardware or software to function differently than you would expect. The bottom line is that bugs can cause you hours and hours of headaches when you are programming.

Bugs of many different types can creep into your programming code. These typically fall into only a few categories, however:

- Syntax-related
- Logic-related
- Operation-related

Syntax-Related Errors

Just as grammar is important in ensuring what you say is understood by other people, *syntax* is vital in making VBA understand what you want done by the computer. Like your ever-watchful mother and father correcting your use of "ain't" and other grammatical mistakes, VBA flags you when it doesn't understand your use of its language. This flagging generally occurs when you attempt to run the program.

Correct syntax, however, doesn't guarantee a working program—at least not if "working" means that the program performs the intended task. Consider the following, grammatically correct, sentence.

```
The far off chickens meow as the blinding flash of darkness settles.
```

What? Chicken meow? Blinding darkness? This is nonsense. Yet, it complies with the grammatical requirements of English. In the same way, you can write syntactically correct programs for VBA that have the same chance of executing properly as the sentence above has of being understood.

Syntax errors are relatively easy to fix, particularly because VBA helpfully points out where the error occurred and gives you a bit of information to help understand what is happening.

Logic-Related Errors

Logic, in computers, typically means the process and order in which tasks are accomplished. For example, you may want to display information on-screen about the contents of a file. It appears that the records display properly, but for some reason, the subtotals don't come out right. Chances are good that this is a logic error—there is something wrong in the code that is causing the wrong figures to add up.

Logic errors can be the most tedious and troublesome errors to find and correct. This is because you typically have to take a "larger approach" view of your program, trying to figure out what happened where and why.

Operation-Related Errors

Operation-related errors are closely related to logic errors, but there are some subtle differences. Operation errors are the kind that generally result from surpassing the limits of the tools you are using. For example, suppose you have written a program and one of the following occurs:

- You exceed the storage capability of a variable.
- You attempt to do a division and the divisor is zero.
- You surpass the precision of a data type.

Each of these results in incorrect data being used, and the second one results in an error when it is encountered. These types of errors can be detected and compensated for, however, if you think through how your program is to be used.

Why are Bugs a Problem?

The manufacturer of a computer goes through several major steps to get the machine into your hands.

1. Design of the computer.
2. Placement of components upon circuit boards.
3. Attachment of circuit boards and other subsystems (power supply, disk drives, and so on) to the chassis and interconnection with other components.
4. Shipping to the vendor.

Whereupon you can purchase your computer.

At any step along the way you can encounter a defect that may render your new machine inoperable. If your computer isn't designed properly, it will never work. If the parts were plugged into the wrong locations on the circuit board, you'll need a new one. If the power supply wasn't wired to the circuit board properly, you'll probably need a whole new machine.

Suppose a part was misplaced in step 2. If there wasn't any testing along the way, all the other labor and material that goes into the computer is worthless. The machine won't work and the manufacturer incurs significant cost in replacing it.

But if the circuit board is tested immediately after part insertion (as they are), the mistake would be found and corrected at a time when the cost is minimal.

As a general rule of thumb, mistakes that go uncorrected cost ten times as much to fix at the next major processing step. If two steps are skipped before the mistake is caught then the cost is 100 times what it would have been had it been corrected immediately. This is why testing occurs at each major step of most manufacturing processes.

The time it takes you to fix a bug in your program works exactly the same way. If you have an error in your basic design you might have to redo the entire application. The time expense in this case is enormous. If you mistype something in a code module and have to track it down after the entire program is complete, it's not as bad as a design flaw. But it can still be time consuming, especially when you consider that most of these errors are avoidable.

So, before you learn about the techniques for removing bugs, it is only appropriate that you review some steps to help prevent them from occurring in the first place.

Keeping Bugs Out

You have already been introduced to several good practices for keeping bugs out of your programs in this book. Because they are so important, take a moment to review them and learn about a few new ones.

- **Use meaningful variable names.** When you are concentrating on programming, it is easy to forget what a variable named J or K2 is for. It takes much less effort to recall the purpose of a variable called iOuterLoopCounter or iMaxCharsPerLine. Every little bit helps and the less you need to concentrate on what a variable is used for, the more you can concentrate on how you are using it.

- **Declare all variables.** Explicit declaration prevents errors due to misspelling. It also guards against another error—data-type confusion. When a variable is undeclared, it most often assumes the type of Variant. Because Variants can hold almost anything, you won't get an error when you assign a string value to a Variant that you intended only to hold numbers or vice versa.

- **Keep procedures short.** Each Function and Sub procedure should perform one specific task—no more and no less. If you fit all the code in a procedure on-screen at once, it is easier to understand. Again, the fewer details, the more you can concentrate on the real task.

- **Test functionality as you go.** Like the manufacturing example given earlier in the chapter, much of your code serves as a basis for later programming stages. By testing each function and subroutine independently, you can isolate errors that, when fixed immediately (while the code is fresh in your mind), aren't terribly expensive to fix. If you don't find the error for a day or more, you may have forgotten how the code functions and you'll need to spend valuable time recalling its purpose. If the error isn't found until after other code has built upon that procedure, there is the chance that you not only need to modify the routine in which the error appears, but also those that use it. Catch and fix your mistakes as early as possible.

- **Verify your design before programming.** If your algorithms are faulty to begin with, no amount of programming can fix them. Even though you are probably anxious to implement your ideas and start coding immediately, resist this temptation. The number of errors that are tracked to faulty logic is surprising. This type of error is very costly to fix because often most of the program must be rewritten.

- **Add meaningful comments to your procedures.** Even if your program works correctly now, at some time in the future you may want to add features, or someone else may be charged with maintaining it. Code without useful comments is like a jigsaw puzzle—a challenge, at best. Commenting your code is like writing assembly instructions on the pieces of the puzzle—they make life much easier. It is good to comment the purpose of each procedure. Usually a line or two at the beginning describing what values are expected, what the routine does, and what, if any, values are returned.

What is Debugging?

As you learned earlier in the chapter, debugging is the process of removing bugs from your program. How hard it is to get rid of errors depends on many things: the complexity of your program, the variability of your data, the design process you went through, and your temperament.

Many people say that debugging is actually an art. There is an element of truth in this, because programming is also an art. Some people can sit down in front of a computer, look at code, and immediately comprehend what is wrong. Others can labor for hours, staring at the same code over and over before getting a glimpse of what the problem is.

A programmer is also, by nature, a debugger—you have to be. After all, you understand your programming code more intimately than anyone else. You are not left to fend for yourself, however. VBA provides a series of tools that you can use to debug your macros. The balance of this chapter helps you understand what those tools are and how you can use them in your debugging efforts.

Getting Rid of Bugs

Even if you exercise all the precautions mentioned earlier in this chapter, it always seems that somehow bugs still manage to get through the cracks. This has nothing to do with experience or effort; it simply seems to be a fact of life. Thus, you need to learn how to use the VBA debugging tools—it is inevitable.

When it comes to debugging, the best teacher is experience. In that vein, you should "learn by doing." With that in mind, let's try a short little program that puts information into a Word document. Open a new document (you should only have the one document open) and then press **ALT+F11**. This displays the Visual Basic Editor. Make sure you have a single procedure, like this:

```
Sub TestingMacro()
    Dim MyVar1 As String
    Dim MyVar2 As String
    Dim J As Integer

' The following is the first portion of the test
    MyVar1 = 5
```

```
    MyVar2 = 7
    Selection.TypeText MyVar1 + MyVar2

' The following is the second portion of the test
    For J = 10 To 1
        Selection.TypeText J
    Next J
End Sub
```

Don't be alarmed if, as you are entering this code, you see bugs right away—they are supposed to be there. You learn how to use the tools to uncover and remove these bugs.

The first portion of the test is supposed to add the numbers stored in MyVar1 and MyVar2 and then insert them into your document. The second portion of the test is supposed to count down from 10 to 1, putting each number into the document.

Now run the TestingMacro and take a look at what you see in the document. What's this? You immediately notice that the program gives the wrong result:

You are trying to add the numbers 5 and 7, which should result in 12, but you get 57 displayed. Something is very wrong; there must be a problem with the logic. In addition, the numbers 10 through 1 should appear on the next lines of the document, but they don't. There must be something wrong here, as well.

You could try to analyze the code you've written to determine what is wrong, but that may not be fruitful since you wrote the code in the first place and it obviously isn't working. Let's see what the Visual Basic Editor has in its bag of debugging tricks to help out. After you have a few more tools to work with, you can attack the bugs in this project.

Single Stepping

One of the primary reasons computers are such powerful tools is that they can execute thousands of instructions each second. This ability gives them the blindingly fast speed necessary tasks that would otherwise take you hours, or perhaps days.

If your program isn't behaving the way you expected, this speed can present a problem. How do you isolate a bug to a particular area of your program if thousands of lines are zinging by every second? There is no way for you to see what is happening.

Single stepping is part of the solution to this problem. As its name implies, single stepping lets you step through your program one line at a time. To single step, in the Visual Basic Editor select Single Step from the Debug menu or press **F8**. The first line of code in your program is executed and the program pauses, awaiting your next command. Press the **F8** key again and the next line of your code is executed. You can tell which line is ready to be executed because it appears in yellow. You should press the **F8** key a total of four times; your screen appears as shown in Figure 15-1.

After each press of **F8** your program is paused. When paused, the program is neither terminated nor running. It isn't executing, but it hasn't been unloaded from memory. One of the most advantageous things you can do when a VBA program is paused is examine memory variables.

What's Its Value?

When a program is paused (you are single stepping through it), you can examine the value of variables contained in the current procedure. Variables in other procedures are not visible unless they have been declared as Global variables (see Chapter 2).

You should already be single stepping through your program, as described in the previous section. You've executed the first two lines of your program, where the values of MyVar1 and MyVar2 are set. Your program is now waiting for you to do something.

Chapter 15: Debugging and Error Handling

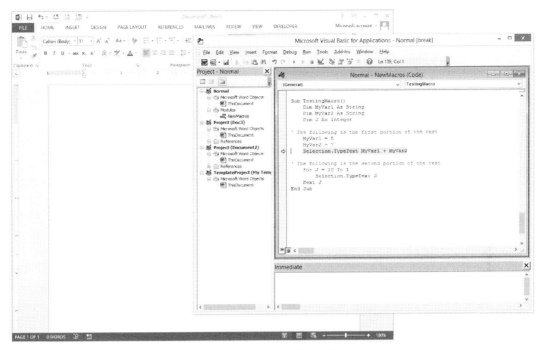

Figure 15-1. Single stepping through your program.

The line that is highlighted in the Code window is the next line that will be executed. Remember the problem from when you first ran the program? The number 57 appeared in your document instead of the number 12, as it should have. Let's look at the variables and see if we can determine why.

Hover the mouse pointer over the variable name MyVar1 in the highlighted line. After a short time you should see a ToolTip appear, telling you the value of MyVar1 ("MyVar1 = 5"). You can also hover the mouse pointer over MyVar2 and see its value.

Now, using your mouse select the words *MyVar1 + MyVar2* in the Code window. Choose Debug | Quick Watch or press SHIFT+F9. You see a small Quick Watch window displayed, as shown in Figure 15-2. This window contains the expression you are evaluating (in the Expression box) and its current value (in the Value box).

Word VBA Guidebook

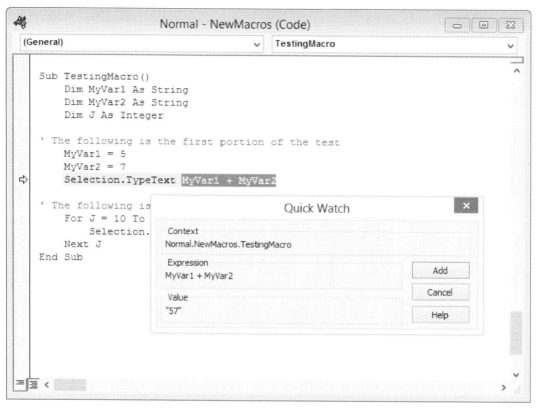

Figure 15-2. A Quick Watch window shows you the value of an expression.

The value of the expression in the Quick Watch window shows that the two values are concatenated; they are not added as expected. Apparently there is something wrong with the formula, even though the individual variables in the formula are correct. Ahh! You have narrowed your problem down to a logic error in your formula.

Because there is only one operator in this formula (the plus sign), it is easy to find the problem. The next step is to look in the on-line help to discover how the plus operator is supposed to work. Press **F1** to display the help system and after a bit of poking around you can discover that if the operands (MyVar1 and MyVar2) are strings, the plus sign concatenates them. The problem your program is exhibiting is that it is interpreting the numbers you have entered as strings and therefore isn't adding them. (This makes sense since you defined the variables as strings in the program.

To fix this problem and make the plus sign work like you want it to, you must be using numeric values. The way to do this is change the variable declarations so that they are using a numeric data type. To make this change, stop your program (remember, it is still paused) by clicking Run | Reset. Then, change the first two lines of the program so they look like this:

```
Dim MyVar1 As Integer
Dim MyVar2 As Integer
```

Now you can run the program and verify that what you see in the document is correct:

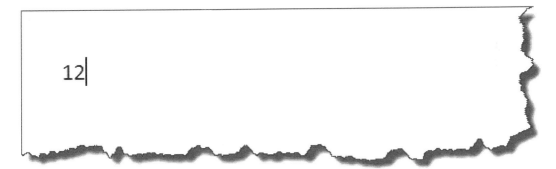

The output from the first portion of the test is now correct, but there is still no output from the second portion of the test.

Stepping By Procedures

So far you have learned how to single step through your program and examine variables, an immense aid in determining where something has gone wrong. You can figure out (by hand, if necessary) what value a variable should contain at a certain point in the program and you can compare that with the value it actually contains. If the two are different, you can backtrack and determine where things went wrong.

While you are single stepping through a procedure, you may come across a program line that calls another procedure. If you continue single stepping by pressing **F8** you see the code for that procedure and single step through it as well. If you are confident the error does not lie in the procedure, you may not want to do this. You want to skip that procedure, instead of executing right through it. VBA allows you to do this by using a *procedure step*.

Procedure steps execute procedures at full speed. They don't skip the procedure; they just run it at its normal speed, which usually results in an immediate return. To step by (or *step over*) a procedure, use **SHIFT+F8**. If the next line of code is not a procedure call, the procedure step button behaves as a single step.

Breakpoints

Stepping through your program a line at a time can quickly become tedious—particularly if you have to step through large amounts of code that have already been tested. Even stepping a procedure at a time can be time consuming in a large macro. Isn't there a way to get right to the source of the suspected problem? Yes! This is why VBA allows you to set breakpoints.

A *breakpoint* is a setting you assign to a line of code that pauses the execution of your program when the line is encountered. A breakpoint is different from an End statement. End terminates the execution of your program and removes it from memory. A breakpoint temporarily pauses your program, allowing you to probe memory and then continue on from the point at which you broke execution.

Breakpoints are a convenience; they allow you to execute your program up to a certain point at full speed. You can then examine the value of variables and step a line, or a procedure, at a time to observe your program's behavior.

Setting a Breakpoint

Setting a breakpoint is easy. While your program is stopped or paused, just position the cursor on the line at which you want VBA to stop. Now click Debug | Toggle Breakpoint or press **F9**. That line appears highlighted in red, meaning that the breakpoint has been set.

When you later run the program and VBA encounters the line at which you have set a breakpoint, it does three things:

- Pause the program
- Display the Code window containing the procedure with the breakpoint
- Wait for your command

At this point, you can apply any other debugging tool you want so you can determine where the error lies.

You should note that when VBA pauses due to encountering a breakpoint, it doesn't execute the line at which it stops. That line is the next line to be executed.

Debugging Using Breakpoints

If you use a breakpoint in conjunction with single stepping, you can see why the second part of the test isn't working properly. Set a breakpoint on the first executable line in the second portion; it is the line on which the For loop starts.

Now run your program. VBA shows the Code window containing the breakpoint, as shown in Figure 15-3. Use the single step tool to start through the procedure. The first thing you notice is that VBA stepped right over the For loop in your code. How could that happen? If you examine the first line closely, applying the information you learn in Chapter 7, you see that the J counter (used in the For loop) starts with the value 10 and that the next value in the loop is 11. What you intended, however, was for it to count backwards, from 10 to 1.

Aha! The problem seems to be that you forgot the Step -1 portion of the For loop, which would have made that happen. Add Step -1 to the statement at the start of the loop, and it works as expected. You can single step through to see that each value is inserted in the document:

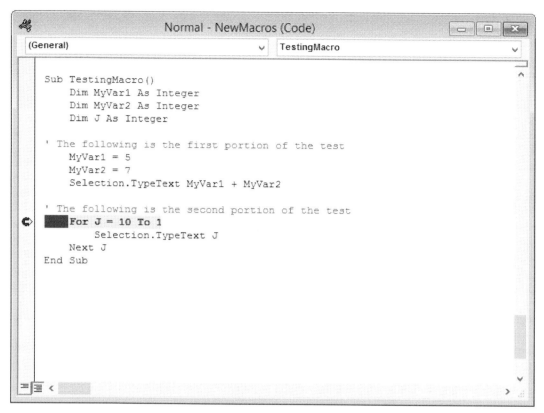

Figure 15-3. VBA stops when it reaches a breakpoint in your code.

There is still a problem, though—all the numbers (10 through 1) are bunched up on a single line. What you wanted to have happen was for each number to be on its own line. Examining the code, again, and applying what you learn in Chapter 11 about editing text using the Selection object, you discover that you need to explicitly add the code for a new line. Change the code to add two lines. It should look like this:

```
Sub TestingMacro()
    Dim MyVar1 As Integer
    Dim MyVar2 As Integer
    Dim J As Integer

' The following is the first portion of the test
    MyVar1 = 5
    MyVar2 = 7
    Selection.TypeText MyVar1 + MyVar2
    Selection.TypeParagraph
```

```
' The following is the second portion of the test
    For J = 10 To 1 Step -1
        Selection.TypeText J
        Selection.TypeParagraph
    Next J
End Sub
```

The next step is to run the program at full speed to make sure it works properly. Before you can do this, however, you must remove the breakpoint. If you don't, then VBA dutifully stop each time it comes to the beginning of the second portion of the test.

To remove a breakpoint, stop your program and position the cursor on the line that contains the breakpoint. Then, click Debug | Toggle Breakpoint or again press **F9**. When you do, the breakpoint (and the tell-tale highlight) is removed.

After the breakpoints are removed, you can run your program at full speed. The output in the document should look just as you expected at the beginning.

Watch Expressions

Earlier you learned how you can use the Quick Watch window to examine the contents of a variable or the results of an expression while your program is running. What if you want to watch the value over the course of the entire program, however? Continually selecting the Quick Watch tool could get very tedious. Fortunately, VBA allows you to set watches to help with this need.

Setting a watch, which in many ways is similar to setting a breakpoint, allows you to monitor the value of any variable in your program. Both the variable name and its value are continually shown in the Watch window. To set a watch expression, select the variable to watch by highlighting it. Then click Debug | Add Watch. You then see the Add Watch dialog box, shown in Figure 15-4.

The Add Watch dialog box allows you to modify exactly what VBA does while it watches the variable. If you only want to continually monitor the value of the variable, you can simply click the OK button. The variable you selected is added to the list of watch values. You can add more if you want.

If you run your program, the name of the variable appears in the Watch window. (You display the Watch window in the Visual Basic Editor by clicking View | Watch Window.)

Breaking on Watches

If you set a breakpoint inside the loop, your program breaks each time the breakpoint is encountered. By using watches, however, you can cause VBA to

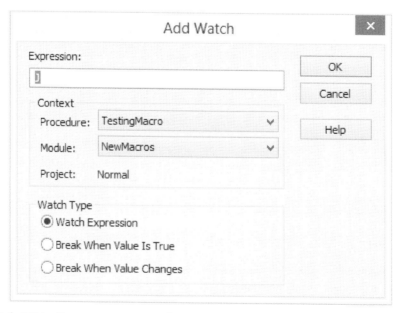

Figure 15-4. *VBA allows you to set watches that monitor variables and expressions for you.*

break the loop only when the loop counter has reached a particular value. This approach is much more efficient when debugging. To see how it works, stop your program and follow these steps:

1. In the Code window, highlight the J variable in the start of the For loop.
2. Choose Debug | Add Watch. The Add Watch dialog box appears, as shown earlier in Figure 15-4.
3. In the Expression text box, enter a formula that defines when you want the program stopped. For example, you can enter the formula J = 4.
4. In the Watch Type box at the bottom of the dialog box, select the Break When Expression Is True option.
5. Click OK.

The watch has now been added. If you run your program you'll find that VBA pauses and enters Debug mode when the loop is encountered and J reaches 4.

Editing a Watch

As you are debugging your programs, it is not unusual to set a watch expression and then later need to change it. For example, you may decide that you want your macro to break when a particular variable contains the value 125 instead of 80. To edit a watch, just select the Edit Watch option from the Debug menu. You then see a list of watch expressions that have been set in your program. You can select any of the watches and click Edit to make your desired changes.

Index

Note: Page numbers with an *f* indicate a figure.

Symbols

! (apostrophe, indicates a comment), 23
\ (backslash operator, integer division), 28
^ (caret character), 28
… (ellipsis points), 59
= (equal operator), 29
/ (forward slash operator, for normal division), 28
\> (greater than operator), 29
\>= (greater than or equal operator), 29
(hash mark or number sign), 26
< (less than operator), 29
<> (not equal operator), 29
. (period, denote movement through object model), 40
" (quotation marks, for string operators), 32

– A –

Abort button, 138
Abort, Retry, and Ignore button, 136
Abs function (positive numbers), 104
accessing functions
    bookmarks, 163–164
    paragraph text, 153–154
access keys, 58–59
ActiveDocument object, 148
AddBiDiMarks (SaveAs and SaveAs2 parameter), 168
adding functions
    bookmarks, 162–163
    documents, 148–149
    information to tables, 189–190
    paragraphs, 152–153
    Quick Access Toolbar, 74–75, 75–76*f*
    Ribbon tabs, 76–78, 77*f*
    tables, 184–185
    text, 176–177, 179–180
    Word interface, 73–74
AddToRecentFiles (document parameter), 150
AddToRecentFiles (Save and SaveAs2 parameter parameter), 167
Alignment (ParagraphFormat object property), 157
AllCaps (Font object property), 160
AllowSubstitutions (SaveAs and SaveAs2 parameter), 168
A<small>LT</small> keys, 57–58
A<small>LT</small>+F8 (display Macro dialog box), 47, 48*f*
A<small>LT</small>+F11 (display Visual Basic Editor), 2, 3*f*
A<small>LT</small>+Q, close VB Editor and return to Word option, 10
American Standard Code for Information Interchange. *See* ASCII
And, logical operator, 30
apostrophe (!), indicates a comment, 23

Application object, 36
arithmetic operators, 28
arrays
    changing on the fly, 125–126
    getting information about, 127
    memory consumed by, 127–128
    multidimensional, 126–127
    overview, 123–124
    setting up, 124–125
Asc function (convert single character), 96
ASCII (American Standard Code for Information Interchange)
    defined, 94, 202
    reading text files, 208–209
    writing to text files, 209–210
AutoClose, 52
AutoExec, 52
AutoExit, 52
automatic macros, 51–52
AutoNew, 51–52
AutoOpen, 52

– B –

backslash operator (*), integer division, 28
BaseLineAlignment (ParagraphFormat property), 157
base two numbering system, 93–94
BeforeRow (table parameter), 186
binary files
    determine current position in, 218
    opening, 216
    overview, 216
    reading from, 217
    updating current position in, 217–218
    writing to, 217
binary numbering system, 93–94
Bold (Font object property), 160
bookmarks, 161–165
Boolean data type, 25
border set, 117
Borders (Font object property), 160
Borders (ParagraphFormat property), 157
breakpoints, 230–233, 232f

bugs. See also debugging
    defined, 219
    identifying, 224–225
    overview, 221–222
    preventing, 206, 222–223
    types of, 220–221
built-in commands, 53–54, 53f
built-in dialog boxes, 141–145, 143f
built-in functions, 85
buttons, modifying, 75, 76f, 136
byte data type, 25

– C –

calculations, using variables for, 24
Cancel button, 136, 138, 139
caret character (^), 28
Case clauses, 113
Case Else clause, 113
CDate function, 26
cells, merging and splitting, 186–187, 188f
characteristic changes to tables, 187–189
characters, formatting, 159–161
Chr function (converts number to character), 96
class modules, 16
ClearFormatting method, 193
Close method, 165–166
Close statement, 207–208
closing VB session, 10, 70–71
Code window, 62–64, 63f
Collapse method, 178–179
collections of objects. See objects and collections of objects
ColorIndex (Font object property), 160
columns in tables
    adding, 186
    changing width, 188
    deleting, 185
comments, 22–23, 223
comparison operators, 28–29
CompatibleMode (SaveAs and SaveAs2 parameter), 168
concatenate (combine) strings together, 32, 228

Index

conditional executions
    formatting If...Then structures, 110–111
    If...Then statements, 108–112
    For Loop statement, 114–117
    overview, 107–108
    Select Case structure, 112–113
    Switch statement, 113–114
    using Not with If...Then, 111–112
ConfirmConversions (document parameter), 150
constants, 41–42
Const, keyword statement, 41–42
constructs, 114
containers. *See* Project Explorer
continuing lines, 23–24
copying macro to text file, 83
counter, looping structure, 115–116
counting, 127–128
creating macros, 7–10
CTRL+G (display Immediate Window), 64
CTRL+H (Replace tab in Find and Replace dialog box), 7
CTRL+P (Print menu), 58–59
CTRL+R (display Project Explorer), 49
currency data type, 25
current position, determining in binary files, 218
current time, 89
Customize Ribbon dialog box, 3–4
customizing, 67–70, 68*f*, 70*f*, 75
custom ribbon button, for running macros, 11

– D –

database, defined, 212
data files
    binary files, 216–218
    closing, 207–208
    defined, 201
    file access types, 208–218
    foreign file formats, 203
    import/export formats, 204
    opening, 201
    overview, 201–202
    preventing bugs in, 206
    random-access files, 212–216
    reading, 206–207
    sequential files, 208–212
    text files, 202–203
Data Interchange Format (.DIF), 204
data structures
    arrays, changing on the fly, 125–126
    arrays, getting information about, 127
    arrays, multidimensional, 126–127
    arrays, setting up, 124–125
    arrays, understanding, 123–124
    counting, 127–128
    overview, 123
    user-defined data types, 25–27, 128–129
data types, 25–27, 128–129
DateAdd function (date in the future), 93
DateDiff function (days between two dates), 92
Date function (current date), 88–89
date functions
    data type, 25, 26
    deriving a date, 93
    differences between two dates, 92–93
    extracting part of date, 90
    function overview, 86–87
    getting both time and date, 89–90
    range of dates supported, 88, 88*f*
    storing times and dates, 87–88
    today's date, 88–89
    weekday name, 91
DateSerial function, 26
Day function (day portion of date), 90
debugging
    breakpoints, 230–233, 232*f*
    bugs, defined, 219
    bugs, overview, 221–222
    bugs, types of, 220–221
    defined, 219
    identifying bugs, 224–225
    Immediate Window, 64
    logical-related errors, 220
    operation-related errors, 221
    overview, 224
    preventing bugs, 206, 222–223
    single stepping, 226–230, 227–228*f*
    syntax-related errors, 220
    tools for, 226–235
    trap and identify file errors, 206
    watch expressions, 233–235, 234*f*
decimal data type, 25

declaring an array, 125, 127
declaring variables, 26, 223
default input parameter (MsgBox), 140–141, 140f
deleting functions
    bookmarks, 165
    columns in tables, 185
    macros, 13
    paragraphs, 154
    rows in tables, 185
    tables, 190
    text, 177–178, 181
delimited text files, 204, 211–212
design of program, 223
Developer tab, Visual Basic Editor, 2–4
dialog boxes, 141–145, 143f. See also MsgBox statement
.DIF (Data Interchange Format), 204
Dim keyword, 26
Dim statement, 124–125
Disable all macros except digitally signed macros (security setting), 7
Disable all macros with notification (security setting), 6
Disable all macros without notification (security setting), 6
discrete actions, 9
division operators, 28
Docking tab (Options dialog), 69
DOCM (regular Word document with VBA module), 46
Document_BuildingBlockInsert event, 49
Document_Close event, 50
Document_ContentControlAfterAdd event, 50
Document_ContentControlBeforeContentUpdate event, 50
Document_ContentControlBeforeDelete event, 50
Document_ContentControlBeforeStoreUpdate event, 51
Document_ContentControlOnEnter event, 51
Document_ContentControlOnExit event, 51
DocumentDirection (document parameter), 151
Document_New event, 51
Document object
    bookmarks, 164–165
    Close method, 165–166
    creating new, 148–149
    defined, 36
    formatting, 156–161
    naming, 151–152
    opening existing, 149–151
    overview, 147–148
    paragraphs, 152–154
    SaveAs method, 166–168
    Save method, 166
    saving, 165–168
    styles, 155–156
Document_Open event, 51
Documents, storage of, 48
Document_Sync event, 51
Document_XMLAfterInsert event, 51
Document_XMLBeforeDelete event, 51
DOCX (regular Word document), 46
Do Loop clause, 118–120
DoProcessing procedure, 173
DOTM (Word template with VBA module), 46
DOTX (Word template without macros), 46
double data type, 25
DoubleStrikeThrough (Font object property), 160
Duplicate (ParagraphFormat property), 157

– E –

editing functions
    macros, 11–13, 12f
    range, 179–181
    selection, 176–178
    watch expressions, 235
Editor Format tab (Options dialog), 69
Editor tab (Options dialog), 68–69
ellipsis points (...), 59
ElseIf and Else statements, 109–110
EmbedTrueTypeFonts (SaveAs and SaveAs2 parameter), 167
Emboss (Font object property), 160
em-dash, character code, 154
Enable all macros (security setting), 7
Encoding (document parameter), 150
Encoding (SaveAs and SaveAs2 parameter), 167
end-of-file (Eof) function, 209
Engrave (Font object property), 160

ENTER key, 58
enumerations (enum), 42
Envelope object, 39
environment for VBA macros
    code window, 62–64
    customizing, 67–70
    displaying Visual Basic Editor, 55–57, 56f
    help system, 65–67
    Immediate Window, 64
    menu bar, 57–59
    overview, 55
    parts of, 57–64
    program options, 68–69
    Project Explorer, 60–61
    project properties, 69–70, 70f
    properties window, 61–62
    quitting session, 70–71
    toolbar, 59–60
Eof (end-of-file) function, 209
equal (=) operator, 29
Eqv (equivalent), logical operator, 30, 31
Erase statement, 126
Err function, 206
error handling. See debugging
event handlers, 49–51, 50f
exclamation mark icon, 135
exclusive Or (Xor) logical operator, 30, 31
Execute method, 193, 195
existing documents, opening, 149–151
Exit Do statement, 119–120
explicit declaration, 26, 223
exponentiation operator, 28
export formats, 204
exporting macros, 81–83, 82f
extracting functions
    ends and middle of a string, 100
    an integer, 101
    part of date, 90
    part of time, 91–92

– F –

F1 (help system displayed), 33
F8 (single stepping through code), 33
F9 (Toggle Breakpoint), 230, 233

faulty logic, 223
feedback, from users, 137–138, 144
FileFormat (SaveAs and SaveAs2 parameter), 167
filename extensions, 46
FileName (SaveAs and SaveAs2 parameter), 167
files. See data files
FileSave command, 54
Find and Replace dialog box, 7–8
Find object, 191–199
Find properties, 193–195
FirstLineIndent (ParagraphFormat property), 157
Follow method, 38
Font (find property), 193
Font object, 159–161, 188–189
Font (replace property), 198
For Each Loop statement, 117
foreign file formats, 203
For Loop statement, 114–117
Format (document parameter), 150
Format (find property), 194
Format function (formats numbers), 105
formatting
    characters, 159–161
    If...Then structures, 110–111
    indentation code, 110–111
    individual characters, 156
    multi-line form code, 110–111
    numbers, 105
    paragraphs, 156–159
    table changes, 188–189
    tables, 188–189
    using styles, 155–156
Forward (find property), 194
forward slash operator (/), for normal division, 28
FullName property, 151
functionality, testing, 223. See also debugging
function keys, 59. See also shortcut keys
functions
    basic procedure, 19–21
    benefits of, 85–86
    built-in functions, 85
    current time, 89
    date and time overview, 86–87
    date, deriving, 93
    date, extracting part of, 90

differences between two dates, 92–93
formatting numbers, 105
getting both time and date, 89–90
integer extraction, 101
math function overview, 100–101
positive values, 104
random number generator, 101–103
range of dates supported, 88, 88f
sign of a number, 103–104
storing times and dates, 87–88
string comparison, 94–95
string conversion, 95–97
string creation, 98
string function overview, 93–94
string length, 99
strings, extracting ends and middle of, 100
strings within strings, 99–100
subroutines vs., 19
time, extracting part of, 91–92
today's date, 88–89
weekday name, 91

– G –

General tab (Options dialog), 69
Get statement, 215, 217
Global statement, 125
global template (Normal.dotm), 9, 46, 48
GoTo statements, 121
graphic shapes, 36
greater than (>) operator, 29
greater than or equal (>=) operator, 29
green text (indicates a comment), 23
greyed out menu items, 60
grouping similar objects, 36–37

– H –

hash marks (#), 26
Height property (table rows), 188
help system, 33, 34f, 65–67, 66f
Hidden (Font object property), 160
Highlight (find property), 194
Highlight (replace property), 198
hot keys, 57. *See also* shortcut keys
Hyperlink object, 38

Hyphenation (ParagraphFormat property), 157

– I –

icons, modifying, 75, 76f, 135–136, 136f
"i" for information icon, 135
If...Then statements, 108–112
Ignore button, 136, 138
IgnorePunct (find property), 194
IgnoreSpace (find property), 194
Immediate Window, 64
Imp (implication), logical operator, 30, 31
import formats, 204
importing macros, 83–84
incrementing Loop counter, 115–116
indentation code formatting, 110–111
InputBox function
    overview, 138–139, 139f
    prompt parameter, 139–140, 139f
    title parameter, 140
Input function, 206–207
Input # statement, 211
inserting paragraphs, 177
insertion point, 170, 173
InsertLineBreaks (SaveAs and SaveAs2 parameter), 167
InsertParagraphAfter method, 177
InsertParagraphBefore method, 177
InsertParagraph method, 177
InStr function (strings within strings), 99–100
integer data type, 25
integer division, 28
Int function (portion of a number to left of decimal), 101
Italic (Font object property), 160

– K –

KeepTogether (ParagraphFormat property), 157
KeepWithNext (ParagraphFormat property), 157
Kerning (Font object property), 160
keyboard shortcuts. *See* shortcut keys

– L –

LBound functions (determine dimension of an array), 127
LCase function (lower case conversion), 96
Left function (left portion of string), 100
LeftIndent (ParagraphFormat property), 157
Len function (length of string), 99
less than (<) operator, 29
less than or equal (<=) operator, 29
LineEnding (SaveAs and SaveAs2 parameter), 168
Line Input # statement, 209
line numbers, 121
LineSpacing (ParagraphFormat property), 157
LineSpacingRule (ParagraphFormat property), 157
LineUnitAfter (ParagraphFormat property), 157
LineUnitBefore (ParagraphFormat property), 157
literal constants, 41
location for storing macros, 46–48
LockComments (SaveAs and SaveAs2 parameter), 167
Loc statement, 218
Lof function, 207
logical operators, 30–31
logical-related errors, 220
long data type, 25
looping structures
    Do Loop clause, 118–120
    For Each Loop statement, 117
    exiting a Loop, 119–120
    first time through Do Loop, 118–119
    incrementing Loop counter, 115–116
    For Loop statement, 114–117
    nesting For Loop statement, 116–117
    overview, 114
    While loops, 118, 120

– M –

Macro dialog box, 47, 48f
macros
    adding to Quick Access Toolbar, 74–75, 75–76f
    adding to Ribbon tabs, 76–78, 77f
    adding to Word interface, 73–74
    built-in dialog boxes, 141–145, 143f
    buttons, modifying, 75, 76f
    comments in, 22–23
    continuing lines, 23–24
    creating, 7–10
    custom ribbon button, 11
    defined, 1
    deleting, 13
    editing, 11–13, 12f
    enameling, 5–7
    exporting, 81–83, 82f
    importing, 83–84
    message box. See MsgBox statement
    naming. See naming considerations
    Organizer tool, 80–81, 81f
    recording, 7–9, 8f, 46–47, 47f
    running, 10–11
    shortcut keys, 11, 57–59, 78–80, 79f
    writing from scratch, 9–10, 10f, 47–48
Macro Security tool, 5
MatchAllWordForms (find property), 194
MatchCase (find property), 194
MatchPhrase (find property), 194
MatchSoundsLike (find property), 194
MatchWholeWord (find property), 194
MatchWildcards (find property), 194
math functions
    formatting, 105
    integer extraction, 101
    overview, 100–101
    positive values, 104
    random number generator, 101–103
    sign of a number, 103–104
memory
    consumed by an array, 127–128
    freeing, 126
menu bar, VB Editor, 57–59
merging cells, 186–187, 188f
methods, defined, 38
Microsoft Developer Network (MSDN) Library, 33–35, 35f, 67
Microsoft Word objects. See objects and collections of objects
Mid function (middle portion of string), 100
MirrorIndents (ParagraphFormat property), 157
Modify Button dialog box, 75, 76f
modules, defined, 16

modulus operator (Mod), 28
Month function (month portion of date), 90
MoveDown (insertion point), 170
MoveLeft (insertion point), 170
MoveRight (insertion point), 170
MoveUp (insertion point), 170
MSDN (Microsoft Developer Network) Library, 33–35, 35f, 67
MsgBox statement. *See also* dialog boxes
    buttons, modifying, 136
    combining buttons and icons, 137, 137f
    default input parameter, 140–141, 140f
    getting input for, 131–138
    icons, modifying, 135–136, 136f
    message parameters, 132–134, 133–134f
    overview, 132
    prompt parameter, 139–140
    screen coordinates, 141
    as a statement vs. as a function, 137–138
    title parameter, 134–135, 140
    user feedback, 137–138
    user input, 138–141
multidimensional arrays, 126–127
multi-line form code formatting, 110–111

– N –

Name (Font object property), 160
Name property, 151
naming considerations
    automatic macros, 51–52
    built-in commands, 53–54, 53f
    documents, 151–152
    event handlers, 49–51, 50f
    location when creating macros from scratch, 47–48
    location when recording macros, 46–47, 47f
    overview, 43–44
    renaming, 44–45
    storing macros, 45–48
    using meaningful variable names, 222
navigating, Help system, 67
nesting For Loop statement, 116–117
nesting If...Then structure, 110–111
new documents, creating, 148–149
No button, 136, 138

NoEncodingDialog (document parameter), 151
NoLineNumber (ParagraphFormat property), 157
non-document files
    binary files, 216–218
    export formats, 204
    file access types, 208–218
    file basics, 204–205
    file types overview, 201–202
    foreign file formats, 203
    handling file errors, 206
    import formats, 204
    opening a file, 205
    overview, 201
    random-access files, 212–216
    reading ASCII text files, 208–209
    reading binary files, 217
    reading data files, 206–207
    reading delimited text files, 211
    reading from binary access files, 217
    reading records from random-access files, 215
    sequential files, 208–212
    text files, 202–203
    updating current position in binary file, 217–218
    user-defined types, 212–214, 214f
    writing delimited text files, 212
    writing records from random-access files, 215–216
    writing to ASCII text files, 209–210
    writing to binary access files, 217
NoProofing (find property), 194
NoProofing (replace property), 198
Normal.dotm (global template), 9, 46, 48
not equal (<>) operator, 29
Not (or the logical opposite of) logical operator, 30, 31
Not, used with If...Then, 111–112
Now function (current date and time), 89
number signs (#), 26

– O –

object data type, 25, 27
Object List control, 62
object members, 38–40
object-oriented programming language, 16

objects and collections of objects. *See also* arrays; *specific types of object*
    assigning to variables, 37
    bookmarks, 161–162
    defined, 16, 36
    documents, 147–148
    For Each Loop statement, 117
    grouping similar objects, 36–37
    object model, 33–36
    overview, 32
    paragraphs, 152
    tables, 183
OK and Cancel buttons, 136
OK button, 136, 138, 139
On Error Resume Next statement, 206
on-line help system. *See* Help system
OpenAndRepair (document parameter), 151
OpenConflictDocument (document parameter), 151
Open method, 149–151
Open statement, 205, 214, 216
operation-related errors, 221
operations with methods, 38
operators
    arithmetic, 28
    comparison, 28–29
    logical, 30–31
    overview, 24, 27–28
    string, 32
Option Base statement, 127–128
Options dialog box, 68–69, 68*f*
Organizer tool, 80–81, 81*f*
Or, logical operator, 30, 31
Outline (Font object property), 160
OutlineLevel (ParagraphFormat property), 157

– P –

PageBreakBefore (ParagraphFormat property), 157
ParagraphFormat (find property), 194
ParagraphFormat object, 156–159
ParagraphFormat (replace property), 198
Paragraph object
    accessing, 153–154
    adding, 152–153
    deleting, 154
    overview, 152
parameters
    passing to functions, 20–21
    passing to subroutine, 18–19
PasswordDocument (document parameter), 150
Password (SaveAs and SaveAs2 parameter), 167
PasswordTemplate (document parameter), 150
Path property, 151
periods (.), to denote movement through object model, 40
placeholder name, 152
plural object names, 37
Position (Font object property), 160
positive values function, 104
Preserve clause, 126
Print menu (CTRL+P), 58–59
Print # statement, 210
private procedures, 21–22
Procedure List control, 62–63
procedures
    defined, 17–18
    functions, 19–21
    scope, 21–22
    size, 223
    subroutines, 18–19
procedure steps, 230
program flow
    conditional execution, 107–114
    Do Loop clause, 118–120
    For Each Loop statement, 117
    exiting a Loop, 119–120
    formatting If...Then structures, 110–111
    GoTo statements, 121
    If...Then statements, 108–112
    incrementing Loop counter, 115–116
    looping structures, 114–120
    For Loop statement, 114–117
    nesting For Loop statement, 116–117
    overview, 107
    Select Case structure, 112–113
    Switch statement, 113–114
    using Not with If...Then, 111–112
    While loops, 118, 120
    While-Wend clause, 120
programming statements, 39

program options, 68–69, 68f
Project Explorer, 16, 17f, 49, 49–50f, 60–61
Project properties, 69–70, 70f
projects, 16–17, 17f
prompt parameter, 139–140
properties, 38–39
Properties window, 61–62
pseudo-random numbers, 101
public procedures, 21
Put statement, 215–216, 217

– Q –

question mark icon, 135
Quick Access Toolbar, 74–75, 75–76f
Quick Watch window, 227–228, 228f
quitting VB session, 10, 70–71
quotation marks ("), for string operators, 32

– R –

random-access files
    opening, 214
    overview, 212
    reading records from, 215
    user-defined record variables, 212–214
    writing records to, 215–216
random number generator, 101–103
Range object
    adding text, 179–180
    creating, 178–179
    defined, 36
    deleting text, 181
    editing, 179–181
    overview, 169–170
    replacing text, 180–181
readability of code
    comments, 22–23
    continuing lines, 23–24
    multi-line form formatting, 110–111
    Not, used with If...Then statements, 111–112
reading functions
    ASCII text files, 208–209
    binary files, 217
    data files, 206–207

delimited text files, 211
random-access files, 215
ReadOnly (document parameter), 150
ReadOnlyRecommended (SaveAs and SaveAs2 parameter), 167
recording macros, 7–9, 8f, 46–47, 47f, 191–193, 192f
Record Macro dialog box, 7–8, 8f
ReDim statement, 125–126
reference objects, 16
remainder of division operation, 28
renaming macros, 44–45
Replacement object, 197–199
replacing text, 180–181
Require Variable Declaration check box, 69
resizing tables, 186
Retry and Cancel buttons, 136
Retry button, 136, 138
Revert (document parameter), 150
ribbon interface, 2
Rich Text Format (.RTF), 204
Right function (right portion of string), 100
RightIndent (ParagraphFormat property), 158
Rnd function (random number generator), 101–103
row height, changing in tables, 188
rows, adding to tables, 186
rows, deleting from tables, 185
.RTF (Rich Text Format), 204

– S –

SaveAs2 method, 166–167
SaveAsAOCELetter (SaveAs and SaveAs2 parameter), 167
SaveAs method, 166–168
SaveFormsData (SaveAs and SaveAs2 parameter), 167
Save method, 166
SaveNativePictureFormat (SaveAs and SaveAs2 parameter), 167
saving functions (document object), 165–168
Scaling (Font object property), 160

scope, defining, 21–22
screen coordinates parameters, 141
Scroll Bars control, 63
searching, 66–67, 191–197, 192f
security settings, 6–7
Seek statement, 217–218
Select Case structure, 112–113
selection
    adding text, 176–177
    collapsing, 178
    creating, 170–172
    defined, 169
    deleting text, 177–178
    editing, 176–178
    finding information about, 172–176
    general information, 172–173
    inserting paragraphs, 177
    selection information, 173–175
    table information, 175–176
sequential files, 208–212
serial number technique, 26
Set keyword statement, 37
Sgn function (sign of a number), 103–104
Shading (Font object property), 160
Shading (ParagraphFormat property), 158
Shadow (Font object property), 160
Shape objects, 36
SHIFT+6 (exponentiation operator), 28
SHIFT+F8 (step by or over a procedure), 227
SHIFT+F9 (Quick Watch window), 227
shortcut keys, 11, 57–59, 78–80, 79f. *See also* specific keys (e.g. ALT, CTRL, SHIFT)
sign of a number function, 103–104
single data type, 25
single stepping, 64, 99, 226–230, 227–228f
Size (Font object property), 160
Slection object, 36
SmallCaps (Font object property), 160
SpaceAfter (ParagraphFormat property), 158
space and underscore sequence (signifying continuing lines), 23
SpaceBeforeAuto (ParagraphFormat property), 158
SpaceBefore (ParagraphFormat property), 158

Space function (create string of spaces), 98
Spacing (Font object property), 160
spaghetti code, 121
splitting cells, 186–187
statements, programming, 39
Static declaration, 125
stepping by procedures, 229–230
stepping through code, 64, 99, 226–230, 227–228f
Step value, 115–116
stop sign icon, 135
storing macros, 45–48
storing times and dates, 87–88
StrComp function (compares strings), 95
Str function (convert number to string), 97
StrikeThrough (Font object property), 160
string data type, 25
String function (create string of characters all the same), 98
string functions
    case of string, 96
    characters to values conversion, 96
    comparing, 94–95
    converting, 95–97
    creating, 98
    extracting ends and middle of a string, 100
    length of a string, 99
    number to a string conversion, 97
    overview, 93–94
    strings within strings, 99–100
    string to a number conversion, 97
    values to characters conversion, 96–97
string operators, 32
structure changes to tables, 185–187
Style (find property), 194
Style (ParagraphFormat property), 158
Style property, 155–156
Style (replace property), 198
subroutines, 18–19
Subscript (Font object property), 161
Supescript (Font object property), 161
Switch statement, 113–114
symbolic constants, 41–42
syntax-related errors, 220

– T –

tables
    adding information to, 189–190
    cells, merging and splitting, 186–187, 188*f*
    characteristics changes, 187–189
    columns, adding, 186
    columns, deleting, 185
    column width, changing, 188
    creating, 183–185
    deleting, 190
    formatting changes, 188–189
    overview, 183
    row height, changing, 188
    rows, adding, 186
    rows, deleting, 185
    selecting information from, 175–176
    structure changes, 185–187
TabStops (ParagraphFormat property), 158
templates, 46, 48. *See also* Organizer tool
testing, 223. *See also* debugging
TextboxTightWrap (ParagraphFormat property), 158
TextColor (Font object property), 161
text files
    ASCII, 94, 202, 208–210
    delimited, 211–212
    overview, 202–203
Text (find property), 194
Text property (Paragraph object), 153–154
Text (replace property), 198
TextShadow (Font object property), 161
ThisDocument object, 49
time
    current time, 89
    data type, 26
    extracting part of, 91–92
    function overview, 86–87
    getting both time and date, 89–90
    storing times and dates, 87–88
Time function (current time), 89
title parameter
    InputBox function, 140
    MsgBox statement, 134–135
To, keyword, 127
Toolbar, 59–60
ToolTips, 60

Track Changes feature, 173
trailing spaces, 181
trap and identify file errors, 206
Trust Center
    displaying, 5–6, 6*f*
    security settings, 6–7
twips, defined, 141
Type…End Type data structure, 213–214
Type Mismatch error, 135
TypeParagraph method, 177
TypeText method, 176–177, 178

– U –

UBound functions (determine dimension of an array), 127
UnderlineColor (Font object property), 161
Underline (Font object property), 161
Until clause, 118
updating current position in binary files, 217–218
user-defined data types, 128–129
user-defined record variables, 212–214, 214*f*
UserForm objects, 16

– V –

Val function (convert number in string to value), 97
Variable (document parameter), 151
variable names, 222
variables
    data types, 25–27
    declaring, 26, 223
    objects assigned to, 37
    overview, 24
variant data type, 25, 27
vbCrLf (carriage return/line feed) constant, 134
View Controls, 63
Visual Basic Editor
    closing application, 10, 70–71
    code window, 62–64, 63*f*
    customizing, 67–70, 68*f*, 70*f*, 75
    Developer tab, 2–4, 4–5*f*
    displaying application, 55–57, 56*f*
    Immediate Window, 64

menu bar, 57–59
Project Explorer, 60–61
properties window, 61–62
starting application, 2, 3f
toolbar, 59–60
Visual Basic for Applications (VBA), overview, 1–2

– W –

watch expressions, 233–235, 234f
wdActiveEndAdjustedPageNumber (selection information), 173
wdActiveEndPageNumber (selection information), 173
wdActiveEndSectionNumber (selection information), 173
wdAtEndOfRowMarker (table information), 175
wdAutoFitContent (table parameter), 184
wdAutoFitFixed (table parameter), 185
wdAutoFitWindow (table parameter), 185
wdCapsLock (general information selection), 172
wdCell (selection parameter), 171
wdCharacter (selection parameter), 171
wdColumn (selection parameter), 171
wdDialog (dialog box naming convention), 142
wdEndOfRangeColumnNumber (table information), 175
wdEndOfRangeRowNumber (table information), 176
wdExtend (selection parameter), 171
wdFirstCharacterColumnNumber (selection information), 173
wdFirstCharacterLineNumber (selection information), 173
wdFrameIsSelected (selection information), 173
wdHeaderFooterType (selection information), 174
wdHorizontalPositionRelativeToPage (selection information), 174
wdHorizontalPositionRelativeToTextBoundary (selection information), 174
wdInClipboard (selection information), 174
wdInCommentPane (selection information), 174
wdInEndnote (selection information), 174
wdInFootnore (selection information), 174
wdInFootnoteEndnotePane (selection information), 174
wdInHeaderFooter (selection information), 174
wdInMasterDocument (selection information), 174
wdInWordMail (selection information), 174
wdLine (selection parameter), 171
wdMaximumNumberOfColumns (table information), 176
wdMaximumNumberOfRows (table information), 176
wdNumberOfPagesInDocument (selection information), 174
wdNumLock (general information selection), 172
wdOverType (general information selection), 172
wdParagraph (selection parameter), 171
wdReferenceOfType (selection information), 174
wdReplaceAll (Replace parameter), 199
wdReplaceNone (Replace parameter), 199
wdReplaceOne (Replace parameter), 199
wdRevisionMarking (general information selection), 172
wdRow (selection parameter), 171
wdSection (selection parameter), 171
wdSelectionMode (general information selection), 172
wdSentence (selection parameter), 171
wdStartOfRangeColumnNumber (table information), 176
wdStartOfRangeRowNumber (table information), 176
wdVerticalPositionRelativeToPage (selection information), 175
wdVerticalPositionRelativeToTextBoundary (selection information), 175
wdWithinTable (table information), 176
wdWord8TableBehavior (table parameter), 184
wdWord9TableBehavior (table parameter), 184
wdWord (selection parameter), 171
wdZoomPercentage (general information selection), 172
WeekdayName function (name of the weekday), 91

While loops, 118, 120
While-Wend clause, 120
Width property (table column), 188
WindowControl (ParagraphFormat property), 158
Word 2007
    Developer tab, 4–5
    Find object, 191
    help system, 33, 34*f*, 67
    Quick Access Toolbar, 74
    SaveAs method, 166–167
    shortcut keys, 78
    Trust Center, 5–6
Word 2010
    Developer tab, 3–4
    Find object, 191–192
    help system, 33, 34*f*, 67
    Quick Access Toolbar, 74
    Ribbon tab, 76, 77*f*
    SaveAs2 method, 166
    shortcut keys, 78
    Trust Center, 5–6
Word 2013
    Developer tab, 3–4
    Find object, 191–192
    help system, 33–35, 35*f*
    MDS Library, 67
    Quick Access Toolbar, 74
    Ribbon tab, 76, 77*f*
    SaveAs2 method, 166
    shortcut keys, 78
    Trust Center, 5–6
WordBASIC, 1–2
Word commands, storage of, 48

Word interface, adding macros to, 73–74
Word Options dialog box, 4, 4–5*f*
Wrap (find property), 194
wrapping text, 134, 134*f*
WritePasswordDocument (document parameter), 150
WritePassword (SaveAs and SaveAs2 parameter), 167
Write # statement, 212
writing functions
    ASCII text files, 209–210
    binary files, 217
    delimited text files, 212
    macros from scratch, 9–10, 10*f*, 47–48
    random-access files, 215–216

– X –

Xor (exclusive Or), logical operator, 30, 31

– Y –

Year function (year portion of date), 90
Yes and No button, 136
Yes button clicked, 138
Yes, No, and Cancel button, 136

– Z –

zeroth element, 127

Made in United States
Troutdale, OR
02/06/2025

28726576R00151